THE

INTENTIONAL
Living

WORKBOOK

A YEAR OF INCREASING MINDFULNESS

&

LEADING A MORE PURPOSEFUL LIFE

TABLE OF CONTENTS

"MAY YOU LIVE

EVERY DAY

OF YOUR LIFE"

- Jonathan Swift

INTENTIONAL
Living

Do you ever feel like life is just simply happening to you and you yearn not only for some control, but also joy? Is your daily schedule crammed and confused, with no time to savor life's little moments, or even taste the food you hastily eat before running the next errand?

Your journey to peaceful intentionality starts within these pages.

It's okay and completely normal to be occasionally overwhelmed in life, but it is never too much to ask to reclaim some time, energy, productivity and happiness. This workbook is designed to guide you in ways to find small, targeted action steps to do just that. Over time, those small bits of intention develop into purposeful habits and mindful lifestyle changes that will become your everyday life.

It is recommended that you start slow and not put too much pressure on yourself to completely transform every aspect of your life. Change comes over time and is often a series of successes and setbacks. Honest self-assessment and a willingness to put in the work are what will propel you through any rough patches along the journey.

HOW TO USE THIS WORKBOOK

The workbook encompasses an entire year and is divided into thirteen four-week sections, called cycles. This is designed to break the year into manageable pieces that allow for more frequent moments of reflection and assessment. This will let you track your progress with greater ease because you aren't simply looking back after a whole year to see what worked and what didn't, but rather taking some time at the end of each week and every cycle to make any needed adjustments.

You can start your mindfulness journey on any day. It is recommended to start a new week on either a Sunday or Monday, whichever is more comfortable for you, but it is really up to you. The dates are blank to accommodate different start dates and schedules.

Each cycle starts with some words of encouragement and some things to think about during the upcoming weeks. As time moves forward, these initial thoughts move from broad ideas to focus on a particular area of life where you can add intention. These topics are by no means an exhaustive list of where mindfulness can be introduced, but simply a starting point to jumpstart your thoughts about how you can be present in these moments.

If you are so inclined, the mandala drawings that accent the inspirational quotes at the beginning of each cycle can be used as coloring pages. As you take the time to choose a color palette and shade in the different areas, think about the words on the page and how they can be incorporated into living your daily life with intention.

THE MONTHLY TRACKER

The monthly tracker included at the beginning of each cycle is a useful way to keep an eye on your development of healthy habits. While intentionality focuses on being present in the moment, having an idea of how the addition of positive lifestyle changes progress over time is a valuable resource and provides visual encouragement to keep going.

Write what you would like to track during the month in the label section, and then fill in each square as you accomplish them during the day. If you are a visual person, consider adding a color-coding system to the tracker to either add interest or show differences between completion, partial completion, or an intentional day off. Twenty-eight days have been provided on each tracker to correspond with the length of the cycle.

Check out the Resources section at the back of the book for some good ideas to get you started and be sure to add your own in the space provided so that you don't forget something great to try when the time is right. There is also a blank page of monthly trackers for your use. Make a few copies of the page if you need more space or would like to track things in a specific area of life.

It is best to start with just a few things to track over the month and not make them too ambitious. There will be a higher chance of success if you give yourself the grace to start small and build from the confidence you gain once you see some results.

THE WEEKLY WORKBOOK

The weekly workbook sections are the action steps toward a mindful and intentional life. This is where you will take time and write out action steps that you would like to accomplish during the day. Usually this can be done the night before so that planning is already done for the day. This is not a schedule, but rather a list of things to bring intention into your daily life until it becomes second nature.

It is okay not to fill all five lines at the beginning. It is also okay to repeat the same intention for as many days as it is needed. Life isn't about doing something wholly different every day, so treat the moments where you can add intention the same. If you need to put something like "remember to perform relaxation breathing technique three times today" as an action step for an entire cycle, so be it. Once it becomes routine, let it drop from the list, with the understanding that it may need to be added back at a later date.

Approach the assessment areas with honesty. Those evaluation questions and prompts are there to give you a complete picture of your progress. Remember to include any issues or situations that may have contributed to how well you were able to add intention to your life that week as a reminder of what was going on in your life at the time. The follow-up section provides an area to visually represent your stress and productivity levels during the week. Consider productivity as not just how much you got done, but if you found more time available to you because you were able to focus on each moment with intention. An additional line has been added if you would like to monitor something else during the week.

In later cycles, the wellness wheel is also available to help you evaluate balance across many areas of life. There are additional wellness wheels in the Resources section if you would like to copy the page to use one daily or in another notebook.

THE CYCLE ASSESSMENT

The assessment pages at the end of a cycle should be treated the same way as the weekly follow-up. Be honest in your evaluation and purposeful in your future goals. This is how you will continue to see growth in intentionality.

THE RESOURCES

These final few pages in the back of the workbook are designed to give you some intentional living and healthy habit ideas, as well as an area to record some of your own ideas. They are arranged by page according to the areas of life found on the wellness wheel, however, this is not a complete list and more note pages are included as a place to write mindful ideas for other areas of life.

Take what you find useful, disregard what doesn't apply, and add some more ideas as time goes on, with the understanding that some ideas may be implemented later on. Subjects such as finances, raising children, education, and so many more can certainly benefit from daily intentionality, so start a few lists of things in other areas of interest. You'll be surprised at how many little moments of intention you can identify.

One final bit of advice: This workbook is for you....no one else. Certainly seek out other sources of inspiration and help as you move toward your more intentional life, but please remember to not compare yourself to others - your journey is your own and you can do this.

Let's get started!

INTENTIONAL
Living

The Workbook

"THE BEGINNING

IS

THE MOST

IMPORTANT

PART OF THE WORK"

- Plato

INTENTIONAL
Living

IDENTIFYING HEALTHY HABITS

The actionable steps of the weekly pages are just one part to developing an intentional mindset. The addition of healthy habits to your daily routine will support the work you are doing throughout each day.

Identify some healthy habits you would like to incorporate into your mindfulness journey that will help you lead a more purposeful life. Check out the resources section of the workbook if you would like help choosing some healthy habits that have a lot of impact in different areas of life.

Sometimes, these habits may overlap with your daily action steps, and that's okay. There will be times where your intentions for the day don't extend beyond developing these healthy habits, especially at the beginning of your journey.

Keep track each day during the first 4 week cycle on the chart below:

HABIT

28 27 26 25 24 23 22 21 20 19 18 17 16 15 14 13 12 11 10 9 8 7 6 5 4 3 2 1

INTENTIONAL
Living

WEEKLY WORKBOOK

DATE: _____

1. _____
2. _____
3. _____
4. _____
5. _____

DATE: _____

1. _____
2. _____
3. _____
4. _____
5. _____

DATE: _____

1. _____
2. _____
3. _____
4. _____
5. _____

DATE: _____

1. _____
2. _____
3. _____
4. _____
5. _____

DATE: _____

1. _____
2. _____
3. _____
4. _____
5. _____

DATE: _____

1. _____
2. _____
3. _____
4. _____
5. _____

DATE: _____

1. _____
2. _____
3. _____
4. _____
5. _____

Follow Up

NOTES AND THOUGHTS ABOUT THE WEEK:

_____
_____
_____

	0									10
PRODUCTIVITY										
STRESS										
_____										

INTENTIONAL
Living

WEEKLY WORKBOOK

DATE: _____

1. _____
2. _____
3. _____
4. _____
5. _____

DATE: _____

1. _____
2. _____
3. _____
4. _____
5. _____

DATE: _____

1. _____
2. _____
3. _____
4. _____
5. _____

DATE: _____

1. _____
2. _____
3. _____
4. _____
5. _____

DATE: _____

1. _____
2. _____
3. _____
4. _____
5. _____

DATE: _____

1. _____
2. _____
3. _____
4. _____
5. _____

DATE: _____

1. _____
2. _____
3. _____
4. _____
5. _____

Follow Up

NOTES AND THOUGHTS ABOUT THE WEEK:

_____
_____
_____

	0									10
PRODUCTIVITY										
STRESS										
_____										

INTENTIONAL
Living

WEEKLY WORKBOOK

DATE: _____

1. _____
2. _____
3. _____
4. _____
5. _____

DATE: _____

1. _____
2. _____
3. _____
4. _____
5. _____

DATE: _____

1. _____
2. _____
3. _____
4. _____
5. _____

DATE: _____

1. _____
2. _____
3. _____
4. _____
5. _____

DATE: _____

1. _____
2. _____
3. _____
4. _____
5. _____

DATE: _____

1. _____
2. _____
3. _____
4. _____
5. _____

DATE: _____

1. _____
2. _____
3. _____
4. _____
5. _____

Follow Up

NOTES AND THOUGHTS ABOUT THE WEEK:

_____
_____
_____

0   10

PRODUCTIVITY [ ][ ][ ][ ][ ][ ][ ][ ][ ][ ]

STRESS   [ ][ ][ ][ ][ ][ ][ ][ ][ ][ ]

_____   [ ][ ][ ][ ][ ][ ][ ][ ][ ][ ]

INTENTIONAL
Living

WEEKLY WORKBOOK

DATE: _____

1. _____
2. _____
3. _____
4. _____
5. _____

DATE: _____

1. _____
2. _____
3. _____
4. _____
5. _____

DATE: _____

1. _____
2. _____
3. _____
4. _____
5. _____

DATE: _____

1. _____
2. _____
3. _____
4. _____
5. _____

DATE: _____

1. _____
2. _____
3. _____
4. _____
5. _____

DATE: _____

1. _____
2. _____
3. _____
4. _____
5. _____

DATE: _____

1. _____
2. _____
3. _____
4. _____
5. _____

Follow Up

NOTES AND THOUGHTS ABOUT THE WEEK:

_____
_____
_____

	0									10
PRODUCTIVITY										
STRESS										
_____										

19

INTENTIONAL
Living

4 WEEK ASSESSMENT

CONGRATULATIONS! You have completed a 4-week cycle of your journey toward a more intentional life. Now it's time to take an assessment of that time and effort.

it is important to be honest with yourself and understand that this is a long term commitment, not just a short term goal to meet. Allow yourself some grace to grow and develop good practices, while acknowledging the challenges. Success will come in time and look like a healthier, happier you.

WHAT WENT WELL? _____

_____

_____

_____

WHAT WERE SOME CHALLENGES? _____

_____

_____

_____

_____

WHAT ARE SOME WAYS TO OVERCOME AT LEAST ONE CHALLENGE

GOING FORWARD? _____

_____

_____

_____

DID YOU SEE IMPROVEMENTS IN STRESS LEVELS

AND PRODUCTIVITY? _____

_____

ANY ADDITIONAL NOTES AND THOUGHTS :

_____

_____

_____

_____

WHERE WILL YOU FOCUS YOUR INTENTIONS DURING

THE NEXT CYCLE? _____

_____

_____

AFFIRMATION OR QUOTE FOR INSPIRATION

KEEP UP THE GOOD WORK

"START WHERE YOU ARE

USE WHAT YOU HAVE

DO WHAT YOU CAN."

- Arthur Ashe

INTENTIONAL
Living

ESTABLISHING AN ACHIEVABLE ROUTINE

Now that you've identified some healthy habits you want to develop, it's important to spend the time establishing an achievable routine to make sure those good ideas become second nature.

Looking back on the previous month, you might find that some habits were easy to work into daily life, while others were more difficult. This isn't going to surprise you much because a lot of life is the same way. Even if you found that some of the things you chose to try were successful, keep them on the chart again for this month.

Maybe you found that establishing any healthy habit was not very successful. That's okay, too. Allow yourself the grace to say "new month, new start." Keep your list the same but choose a top three to focus on, or reevaluate to identify some habits with a better chance of success if the first choices were a bit too ambitious. None of this is set in stone.

Keep track each day during the second 4 week cycle on the chart below:

HABIT

INTENTIONAL
Living

WEEKLY WORKBOOK

DATE: _____

1. _____
2. _____
3. _____
4. _____
5. _____

DATE: _____

1. _____
2. _____
3. _____
4. _____
5. _____

DATE: _____

1. _____
2. _____
3. _____
4. _____
5. _____

DATE: _____

1. _____
2. _____
3. _____
4. _____
5. _____

DATE: _____

1. _____
2. _____
3. _____
4. _____
5. _____

DATE: _____

1. _____
2. _____
3. _____
4. _____
5. _____

DATE: _____

1. _____
2. _____
3. _____
4. _____
5. _____

Follow Up

NOTES AND THOUGHTS ABOUT THE WEEK:

_____
_____
_____

	0									10
PRODUCTIVITY										
STRESS										
_____										

INTENTIONAL
Living

WEEKLY WORKBOOK

DATE: _____

1. _____
2. _____
3. _____
4. _____
5. _____

DATE: _____

1. _____
2. _____
3. _____
4. _____
5. _____

DATE: _____

1. _____
2. _____
3. _____
4. _____
5. _____

DATE: _____

1. _____
2. _____
3. _____
4. _____
5. _____

DATE: _____

1. _____
2. _____
3. _____
4. _____
5. _____

DATE: _____

1. _____
2. _____
3. _____
4. _____
5. _____

DATE: _____

1. _____
2. _____
3. _____
4. _____
5. _____

Follow Up

NOTES AND THOUGHTS ABOUT THE WEEK:

_____
_____
_____

	0									10
PRODUCTIVITY										
STRESS										
_____										

INTENTIONAL
Living

WEEKLY WORKBOOK

DATE: _____

1. _____
2. _____
3. _____
4. _____
5. _____

DATE: _____

1. _____
2. _____
3. _____
4. _____
5. _____

DATE: _____

1. _____
2. _____
3. _____
4. _____
5. _____

DATE: _____

1. _____
2. _____
3. _____
4. _____
5. _____

DATE: _____

1. _____
2. _____
3. _____
4. _____
5. _____

DATE: _____

1. _____
2. _____
3. _____
4. _____
5. _____

DATE: _____

1. _____
2. _____
3. _____
4. _____
5. _____

Follow Up

NOTES AND THOUGHTS ABOUT THE WEEK:

_____
_____
_____

	0									10
PRODUCTIVITY										
STRESS										
_____										

INTENTIONAL
Living

WEEKLY WORKBOOK

DATE: _____

1. _____
2. _____
3. _____
4. _____
5. _____

DATE: _____

1. _____
2. _____
3. _____
4. _____
5. _____

DATE: _____

1. _____
2. _____
3. _____
4. _____
5. _____

DATE: _____

1. _____
2. _____
3. _____
4. _____
5. _____

DATE: _____

1. _____
2. _____
3. _____
4. _____
5. _____

DATE: _____

1. _____
2. _____
3. _____
4. _____
5. _____

DATE: _____

1. _____
2. _____
3. _____
4. _____
5. _____

Follow Up

NOTES AND THOUGHTS ABOUT THE WEEK:

_____
_____
_____

	0									10
PRODUCTIVITY										
STRESS										
_____										

INTENTIONAL
Living

4 WEEK ASSESSMENT

CONGRATULATIONS! You have completed a 4-week cycle of your journey toward a more intentional life. Now it's time to take an assessment of that time and effort.

it is important to be honest with yourself and understand that this is a long term commitment, not just a short term goal to meet. Allow yourself some grace to grow and develop good practices, while acknowledging the challenges. Success will come in time and look like a healthier, happier you.

WHAT WENT WELL? _____

_____

_____

_____

WHAT WERE SOME CHALLENGES? _____

_____

_____

_____

_____

WHAT ARE SOME WAYS TO OVERCOME AT LEAST ONE CHALLENGE

GOING FORWARD? _____

_____

_____

_____

DID YOU SEE IMPROVEMENTS IN STRESS LEVELS

AND PRODUCTIVITY? _____

_____

SKETCH / BRAIN DUMP / MOOD BOARD AREA

ANY ADDITIONAL NOTES AND THOUGHTS :

_____

_____

_____

_____

WHERE WILL YOU FOCUS YOUR INTENTIONS DURING

THE NEXT CYCLE? _____

_____

_____

AFFIRMATION OR QUOTE FOR INSPIRATION

KEEP UP THE GOOD WORK

"I WALK SLOWLY,

BUT I NEVER

WALK

BACKWARDS."

- Abraham Lincoln

INTENTIONAL
Living

EVALUATE YOUR PROGRESS

Welcome to the third cycle of your journey to live with intentionality! Whether the previous eight weeks went fast or were a struggle, give yourself a moment to appreciate what you've accomplished so far.

This is also a good time to honestly evaluate your progress. Do you see most of the tracker days filled in, or is progress more sporadic? Are your daily intention lists varied, or do you see many of the same ideas repeated? Remember to take a look at other parts of your life during the times you struggle and identify areas to address that may be holding you back. These can be recorded to help clarify any issues on the workbook reflection pages.

Now reflect on your choice of habits to track. Do they all meet more basic physical needs like healthy eating or getting enough sleep, or is there a mix of social/emotional goals included for improvement? Expanding your horizons may be a little bit uncomfortable, but it's how you grow.

Keep track each day during the third 4 week cycle on the chart below:

HABIT

INTENTIONAL
Living

WEEKLY WORKBOOK

DATE: _____

1. _____
2. _____
3. _____
4. _____
5. _____

DATE: _____

1. _____
2. _____
3. _____
4. _____
5. _____

DATE: _____

1. _____
2. _____
3. _____
4. _____
5. _____

DATE: _____

1. _____
2. _____
3. _____
4. _____
5. _____

DATE: _____

1. _____
2. _____
3. _____
4. _____
5. _____

DATE: _____

1. _____
2. _____
3. _____
4. _____
5. _____

DATE: _____

1. _____
2. _____
3. _____
4. _____
5. _____

Follow Up

NOTES AND THOUGHTS ABOUT THE WEEK:

_____
_____
_____

	0									10
PRODUCTIVITY										
STRESS										

INTENTIONAL
Living

WEEKLY WORKBOOK

DATE: _____

1. _____
2. _____
3. _____
4. _____
5. _____

DATE: _____

1. _____
2. _____
3. _____
4. _____
5. _____

DATE: _____

1. _____
2. _____
3. _____
4. _____
5. _____

DATE: _____

1. _____
2. _____
3. _____
4. _____
5. _____

DATE: _____

1. _____
2. _____
3. _____
4. _____
5. _____

DATE: _____

1. _____
2. _____
3. _____
4. _____
5. _____

DATE: _____

1. _____
2. _____
3. _____
4. _____
5. _____

Follow Up

NOTES AND THOUGHTS ABOUT THE WEEK:

_____
_____
_____

	0									10
PRODUCTIVITY										
STRESS										

INTENTIONAL
Living

WEEKLY WORKBOOK

DATE: _____

1. _____
2. _____
3. _____
4. _____
5. _____

DATE: _____

1. _____
2. _____
3. _____
4. _____
5. _____

DATE: _____

1. _____
2. _____
3. _____
4. _____
5. _____

DATE: _____

1. _____
2. _____
3. _____
4. _____
5. _____

DATE: _____

1. _____
2. _____
3. _____
4. _____
5. _____

DATE: _____

1. _____
2. _____
3. _____
4. _____
5. _____

DATE: _____

1. _____
2. _____
3. _____
4. _____
5. _____

Follow Up

NOTES AND THOUGHTS ABOUT THE WEEK:

_____
_____
_____

	0									10
PRODUCTIVITY										
STRESS										
_____										

INTENTIONAL
Living

WEEKLY WORKBOOK

DATE: _____

1. _____
2. _____
3. _____
4. _____
5. _____

DATE: _____

1. _____
2. _____
3. _____
4. _____
5. _____

DATE: _____

1. _____
2. _____
3. _____
4. _____
5. _____

DATE: _____

1. _____
2. _____
3. _____
4. _____
5. _____

DATE: _____

1. _____
2. _____
3. _____
4. _____
5. _____

DATE: _____

1. _____
2. _____
3. _____
4. _____
5. _____

DATE: _____

1. _____
2. _____
3. _____
4. _____
5. _____

Follow Up

NOTES AND THOUGHTS ABOUT THE WEEK:

_____
_____
_____

	0									10
PRODUCTIVITY										
STRESS										

INTENTIONAL
Living

4 WEEK ASSESSMENT

CONGRATULATIONS! You have completed a 4-week cycle of your journey toward a more intentional life. Now it's time to take an assessment of that time and effort.

it is important to be honest with yourself and understand that this is a long term commitment, not just a short term goal to meet. Allow yourself some grace to grow and develop good practices, while acknowledging the challenges. Success will come in time and look like a healthier, happier you.

WHAT WENT WELL? _____

_____

_____

_____

WHAT WERE SOME CHALLENGES? _____

_____

_____

_____

_____

WHAT ARE SOME WAYS TO OVERCOME AT LEAST ONE CHALLENGE

GOING FORWARD? _____

_____

_____

_____

DID YOU SEE IMPROVEMENTS IN STRESS LEVELS

AND PRODUCTIVITY? _____

_____

SKETCH / BRAIN DUMP / MOOD BOARD AREA

ANY ADDITIONAL NOTES AND THOUGHTS :

_____
_____
_____
_____

WHERE WILL YOU FOCUS YOUR INTENTIONS DURING

THE NEXT CYCLE? _____

_____
_____

AFFIRMATION OR QUOTE FOR INSPIRATION

KEEP UP THE GOOD WORK

"SUCCESS IS THE SUM
OF SMALL EFFORTS
REPEATED
DAY IN AND DAY OUT."

- Robert Collier

INTENTIONAL
Living

EXPAND YOUR HORIZONS

Congratulations on completing twelve weeks of tracking healthy habits! Current research suggests that it takes an average of 66 days to fully form a habit. Of course this is widely variable, but if you are sticking to your daily plans of recording your intentional thoughts and tracking healthy habits, hopefully some of these things started to become more routine during the third cycle.

If you feel like you are achieving many of your goals towards increased mindfulness and health, push your boundaries a little bit by replacing a couple of the successful habits you've formed with something more ambitious. Be sure to continue the gains you have made by still doing what you are now good at, but it's okay to make some room on the chart to expand your horizons.

As always, if you are still struggling with developing some healthy habits, focus your attention on a couple of top priorities, and do the best you can.

Keep track each day during the fourth 4 week cycle on the chart below:

INTENTIONAL
Living

WEEKLY WORKBOOK

DATE: _____

1. _____
2. _____
3. _____
4. _____
5. _____

DATE: _____

1. _____
2. _____
3. _____
4. _____
5. _____

DATE: _____

1. _____
2. _____
3. _____
4. _____
5. _____

DATE: _____

1. _____
2. _____
3. _____
4. _____
5. _____

DATE: _____

1. _____
2. _____
3. _____
4. _____
5. _____

DATE: _____

1. _____
2. _____
3. _____
4. _____
5. _____

DATE: _____

1. _____
2. _____
3. _____
4. _____
5. _____

Follow Up

NOTES AND THOUGHTS ABOUT THE WEEK:

_____
_____
_____

	0									10
PRODUCTIVITY										
STRESS										
_____										

INTENTIONAL
Living

WEEKLY WORKBOOK

DATE: _____

1. _____
2. _____
3. _____
4. _____
5. _____

DATE: _____

1. _____
2. _____
3. _____
4. _____
5. _____

DATE: _____

1. _____
2. _____
3. _____
4. _____
5. _____

DATE: _____

1. _____
2. _____
3. _____
4. _____
5. _____

DATE: _____

1. _____
2. _____
3. _____
4. _____
5. _____

DATE: _____

1. _____
2. _____
3. _____
4. _____
5. _____

DATE: _____

1. _____
2. _____
3. _____
4. _____
5. _____

Follow Up

NOTES AND THOUGHTS ABOUT THE WEEK:

_____

_____

_____

	0								10

PRODUCTIVITY

STRESS

_____

INTENTIONAL
Living

WEEKLY WORKBOOK

DATE: _____

1. _____
2. _____
3. _____
4. _____
5. _____

DATE: _____

1. _____
2. _____
3. _____
4. _____
5. _____

DATE: _____

1. _____
2. _____
3. _____
4. _____
5. _____

DATE: _____

1. _____
2. _____
3. _____
4. _____
5. _____

DATE: _____

1. _____
2. _____
3. _____
4. _____
5. _____

DATE: _____

1. _____
2. _____
3. _____
4. _____
5. _____

DATE: _____

1. _____
2. _____
3. _____
4. _____
5. _____

Follow Up

NOTES AND THOUGHTS ABOUT THE WEEK:

_____
_____
_____

0   10

PRODUCTIVITY | | | | | | | | | | |

STRESS | | | | | | | | | | |

_____ | | | | | | | | | | |

INTENTIONAL
Living

WEEKLY WORKBOOK

DATE: _____

1. _____
2. _____
3. _____
4. _____
5. _____

DATE: _____

1. _____
2. _____
3. _____
4. _____
5. _____

DATE: _____

1. _____
2. _____
3. _____
4. _____
5. _____

DATE: _____

1. _____
2. _____
3. _____
4. _____
5. _____

DATE: _____

1. _____
2. _____
3. _____
4. _____
5. _____

DATE: _____

1. _____
2. _____
3. _____
4. _____
5. _____

DATE: _____

1. _____
2. _____
3. _____
4. _____
5. _____

Follow Up

NOTES AND THOUGHTS ABOUT THE WEEK:

_____
_____
_____

	0									10
PRODUCTIVITY										
STRESS										
_____										

INTENTIONAL
Living

4 WEEK ASSESSMENT

CONGRATULATIONS! You have completed a 4-week cycle of your journey toward a more intentional life. Now it's time to take an assessment of that time and effort.

it is important to be honest with yourself and understand that this is a long term commitment, not just a short term goal to meet. Allow yourself some grace to grow and develop good practices, while acknowledging the challenges. Success will come in time and look like a healthier, happier you.

WHAT WENT WELL? _____

_____

_____

_____

WHAT WERE SOME CHALLENGES? _____

_____

_____

_____

_____

WHAT ARE SOME WAYS TO OVERCOME AT LEAST ONE CHALLENGE

GOING FORWARD? _____

_____

_____

_____

DID YOU SEE IMPROVEMENTS IN STRESS LEVELS

AND PRODUCTIVITY? _____

_____

SKETCH / BRAIN DUMP / MOOD BOARD AREA

ANY ADDITIONAL NOTES AND THOUGHTS :

_____

_____

_____

_____

WHERE WILL YOU FOCUS YOUR INTENTIONS DURING

THE NEXT CYCLE? _____

_____

_____

AFFIRMATION OR QUOTE FOR INSPIRATION

KEEP UP THE GOOD WORK

"LIFE IS LIKE RIDING

A BICYCLE

TO KEEP YOUR

BALANCE, YOU MUST

KEEP MOVING."

- Albert Einstein

INTENTIONAL
Living

THE LIFE BALANCE WHEEL

Hopefully you have found some success in establishing healthy habits and mindful routines over the past few weeks. If you are still focusing on a core group of intentions, that is fantastic and keep up the good work!

If you are ready to continue the journey, a new life balance wheel has been added to the weekly assessment area to track how you prioritize different areas of your life. There are eight main focus areas: family & friends, spiritual, work, leisure, exercise, nutrition, hydration and sleep. This is by no means an exhaustive list of life's important points, however, living each of these areas with intention and awareness is important. At the end of each week, fill in an amount of each wedge with a general idea of how much of your time was spent in the different areas. Again, honesty is best and strive for balance in all things.

We will dive deeper into the different life balance areas during the next few cycles, however, you can always check the Resource section now for ideas to add into your daily intentions and habits.

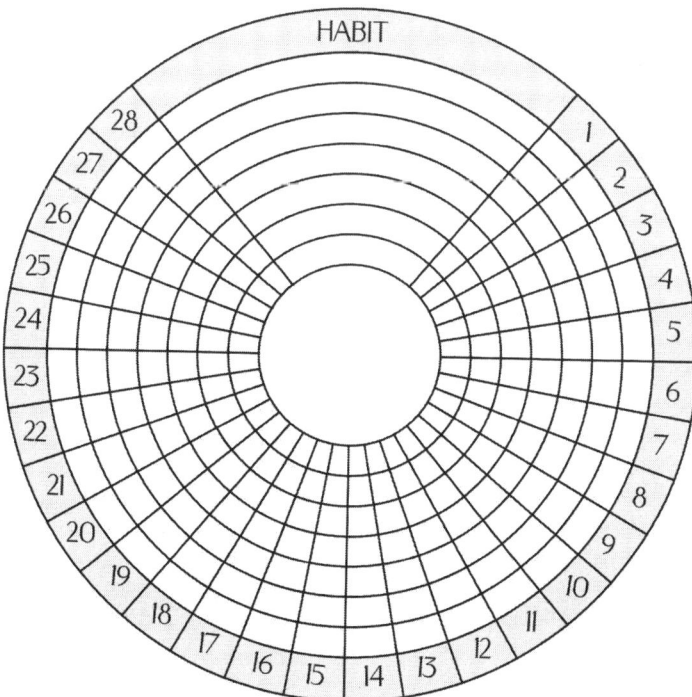
HABIT

INTENTIONAL
Living

WEEKLY WORKBOOK

DATE: _____

1. _____
2. _____
3. _____
4. _____
5. _____

DATE: _____

1. _____
2. _____
3. _____
4. _____
5. _____

DATE: _____

1. _____
2. _____
3. _____
4. _____
5. _____

DATE: _____

1. _____
2. _____
3. _____
4. _____
5. _____

DATE: _____

1. _____
2. _____
3. _____
4. _____
5. _____

DATE: _____

1. _____
2. _____
3. _____
4. _____
5. _____

DATE: _____

1. _____
2. _____
3. _____
4. _____
5. _____

Follow Up

NOTES AND THOUGHTS ABOUT THE WEEK:

_____
_____
_____

LIFE BALANCE

	0	2	4	6	8	10
PRODUCTIVITY						
STRESS						
_____						

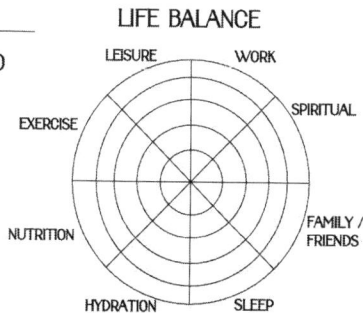

LEISURE   WORK
EXERCISE   SPIRITUAL
NUTRITION   FAMILY / FRIENDS
HYDRATION   SLEEP

INTENTIONAL
Living

WEEKLY WORKBOOK

DATE: _____

1. _____
2. _____
3. _____
4. _____
5. _____

DATE: _____

1. _____
2. _____
3. _____
4. _____
5. _____

DATE: _____

1. _____
2. _____
3. _____
4. _____
5. _____

DATE: _____

1. _____
2. _____
3. _____
4. _____
5. _____

DATE: _____

1. _____
2. _____
3. _____
4. _____
5. _____

DATE: _____

1. _____
2. _____
3. _____
4. _____
5. _____

DATE: _____

1. _____
2. _____
3. _____
4. _____
5. _____

Follow Up

NOTES AND THOUGHTS ABOUT THE WEEK:

_____
_____
_____

LIFE BALANCE

	0	2	4	6	8	10
PRODUCTIVITY						
STRESS						
_____						

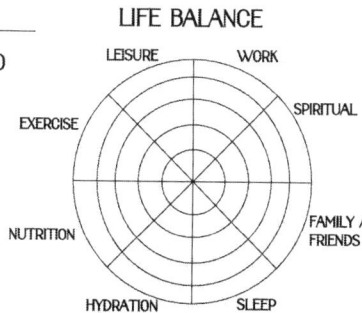

LEISURE WORK SPIRITUAL EXERCISE FAMILY / FRIENDS NUTRITION HYDRATION SLEEP

INTENTIONAL
Living
WEEKLY WORKBOOK

DATE: _____

1. _____
2. _____
3. _____
4. _____
5. _____

DATE: _____

1. _____
2. _____
3. _____
4. _____
5. _____

DATE: _____

1. _____
2. _____
3. _____
4. _____
5. _____

DATE: _____

1. _____
2. _____
3. _____
4. _____
5. _____

DATE: _____

1. _____
2. _____
3. _____
4. _____
5. _____

DATE: _____

1. _____
2. _____
3. _____
4. _____
5. _____

DATE: _____

1. _____
2. _____
3. _____
4. _____
5. _____

Follow Up

NOTES AND THOUGHTS ABOUT THE WEEK:

_____
_____
_____

LIFE BALANCE

	0	2	4	6	8	10
PRODUCTIVITY						
STRESS						

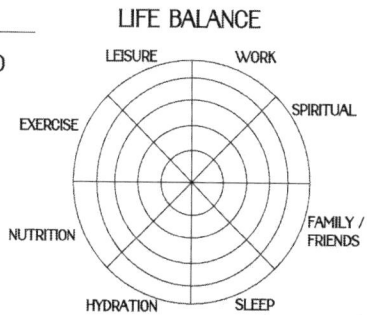

LEISURE — WORK — SPIRITUAL — FAMILY / FRIENDS — SLEEP — HYDRATION — NUTRITION — EXERCISE

INTENTIONAL
Living

WEEKLY WORKBOOK

DATE: _____

1. _____
2. _____
3. _____
4. _____
5. _____

DATE: _____

1. _____
2. _____
3. _____
4. _____
5. _____

DATE: _____

1. _____
2. _____
3. _____
4. _____
5. _____

DATE: _____

1. _____
2. _____
3. _____
4. _____
5. _____

DATE: _____

1. _____
2. _____
3. _____
4. _____
5. _____

DATE: _____

1. _____
2. _____
3. _____
4. _____
5. _____

DATE: _____

1. _____
2. _____
3. _____
4. _____
5. _____

Follow Up

NOTES AND THOUGHTS ABOUT THE WEEK:

_____

_____

_____

LIFE BALANCE

	0	2	4	6	8	10
PRODUCTIVITY						
STRESS						
_____						

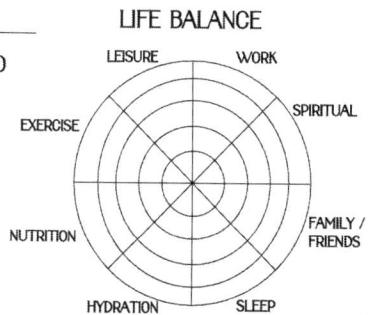

LEISURE   WORK
EXERCISE   SPIRITUAL
NUTRITION   FAMILY / FRIENDS
HYDRATION   SLEEP

INTENTIONAL
Living

4 WEEK ASSESSMENT

CONGRATULATIONS! You have completed a 4-week cycle of your journey toward a more intentional life. Now it's time to take an assessment of that time and effort.

it is important to be honest with yourself and understand that this is a long term commitment, not just a short term goal to meet. Allow yourself some grace to grow and develop good practices, while acknowledging the challenges. Success will come in time and look like a healthier, happier you.

WHAT WENT WELL? _____

_____

_____

_____

WHAT WERE SOME CHALLENGES? _____

_____

_____

_____

_____

WHAT ARE SOME WAYS TO OVERCOME AT LEAST ONE CHALLENGE

GOING FORWARD? _____

_____

_____

_____

DID YOU SEE IMPROVEMENTS IN STRESS LEVELS

AND PRODUCTIVITY? _____

SKETCH / BRAIN DUMP / MOOD BOARD AREA

ANY ADDITIONAL NOTES AND THOUGHTS :

_____

_____

_____

_____

WHERE WILL YOU FOCUS YOUR INTENTIONS DURING

THE NEXT CYCLE? _____

_____

_____

AFFIRMATION OR QUOTE FOR INSPIRATION

KEEP UP THE GOOD WORK

"WELL DONE
IS BETTER THAN
WELL SAID."

- Benjamin Franklin

INTENTIONAL
Living

HIGHLIGHT: FAMILY & FRIENDS

Hopefully the life balance wheel has been helpful for adding intention to your life. Even if it is just giving you a basic idea of where your thoughts have been focused throughout the week, it is a useful tool to help you maintain balance and increase mindfulness.

In this cycle, think about the family and friends aspect a little deeper. No one area is meant to be focused on to the exclusion of the others (remember, balance is important), but these highlights are just to help you examine what each area of the wellness wheel means to you and your intentional life.

Family and friends are a cornerstone of healthy living. Making and maintaining strong bonds with others is one of the ways we are all connected. That sense of connection helps to ground us and keep us accountable. Practicing intention with interpersonal associations can not only strengthen healthy bonds, but also allow you to identify unhealthy aspects of other relationships in your life. Using good habits and intentions are one way to cultivate strong relationships, while identifying areas where distancing is best.

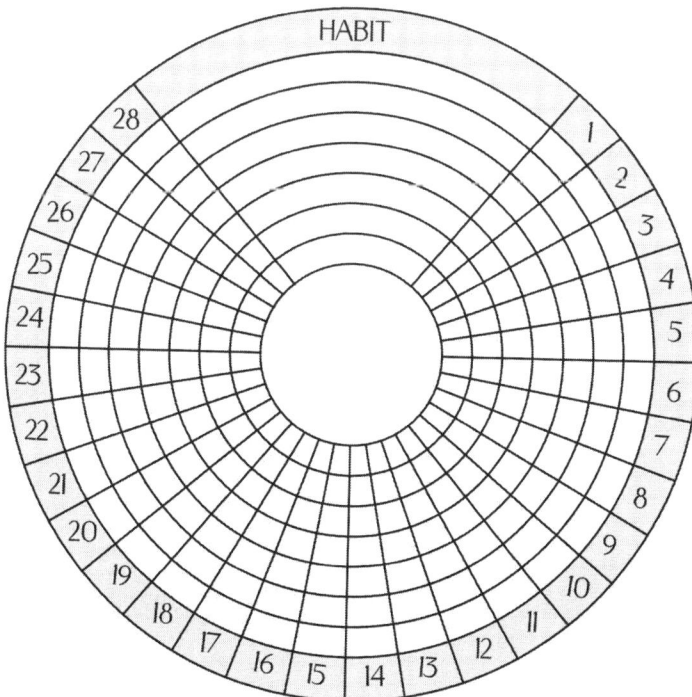

HABIT

28 27 26 25 24 23 22 21 20 19 18 17 16 15 14 13 12 11 10 9 8 7 6 5 4 3 2 1

INTENTIONAL
Living

WEEKLY WORKBOOK

DATE: _____

1. _____
2. _____
3. _____
4. _____
5. _____

DATE: _____

1. _____
2. _____
3. _____
4. _____
5. _____

DATE: _____

1. _____
2. _____
3. _____
4. _____
5. _____

DATE: _____

1. _____
2. _____
3. _____
4. _____
5. _____

DATE: _____

1. _____
2. _____
3. _____
4. _____
5. _____

DATE: _____

1. _____
2. _____
3. _____
4. _____
5. _____

DATE: _____

1. _____
2. _____
3. _____
4. _____
5. _____

Follow Up

NOTES AND THOUGHTS ABOUT THE WEEK:

_____
_____
_____

LIFE BALANCE

	0	2	4	6	8	10
PRODUCTIVITY						
STRESS						
_____						

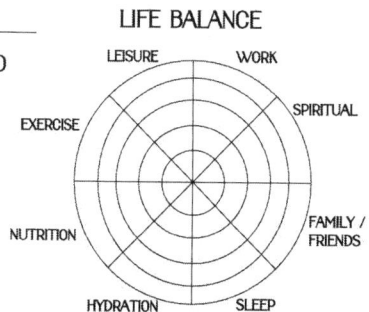

LEISURE · WORK · SPIRITUAL · FAMILY / FRIENDS · SLEEP · HYDRATION · NUTRITION · EXERCISE

INTENTIONAL
Living

WEEKLY WORKBOOK

DATE: _____

1. _____
2. _____
3. _____
4. _____
5. _____

DATE: _____

1. _____
2. _____
3. _____
4. _____
5. _____

DATE: _____

1. _____
2. _____
3. _____
4. _____
5. _____

DATE: _____

1. _____
2. _____
3. _____
4. _____
5. _____

DATE: _____

1. _____
2. _____
3. _____
4. _____
5. _____

DATE: _____

1. _____
2. _____
3. _____
4. _____
5. _____

DATE: _____

1. _____
2. _____
3. _____
4. _____
5. _____

Follow Up

NOTES AND THOUGHTS ABOUT THE WEEK:

_____
_____
_____

LIFE BALANCE

	0	2	4	6	8	10
PRODUCTIVITY						
STRESS						
_____						

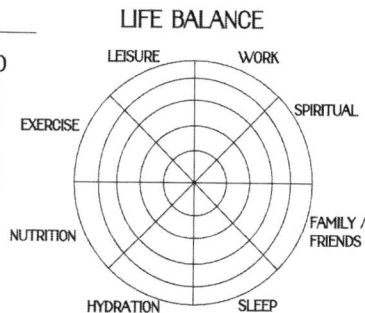

LEISURE WORK
EXERCISE SPIRITUAL
NUTRITION FAMILY / FRIENDS
HYDRATION SLEEP

INTENTIONAL
Living

WEEKLY WORKBOOK

DATE: _____

1. _____
2. _____
3. _____
4. _____
5. _____

DATE: _____

1. _____
2. _____
3. _____
4. _____
5. _____

DATE: _____

1. _____
2. _____
3. _____
4. _____
5. _____

DATE: _____

1. _____
2. _____
3. _____
4. _____
5. _____

DATE: _____

1. _____
2. _____
3. _____
4. _____
5. _____

DATE: _____

1. _____
2. _____
3. _____
4. _____
5. _____

DATE: _____

1. _____
2. _____
3. _____
4. _____
5. _____

Follow Up

NOTES AND THOUGHTS ABOUT THE WEEK:

_____
_____
_____

LIFE BALANCE

	0	2	4	6	8	10
PRODUCTIVITY						
STRESS						
_____						

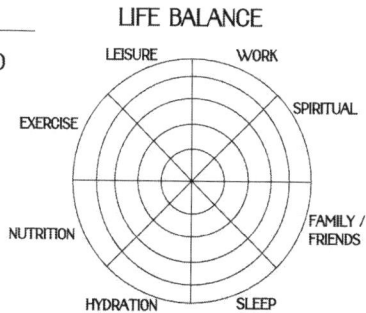

LEISURE · WORK · SPIRITUAL · FAMILY / FRIENDS · SLEEP · HYDRATION · NUTRITION · EXERCISE

INTENTIONAL
Living

WEEKLY WORKBOOK

DATE: _____

1. _____
2. _____
3. _____
4. _____
5. _____

DATE: _____

1. _____
2. _____
3. _____
4. _____
5. _____

DATE: _____

1. _____
2. _____
3. _____
4. _____
5. _____

DATE: _____

1. _____
2. _____
3. _____
4. _____
5. _____

DATE: _____

1. _____
2. _____
3. _____
4. _____
5. _____

DATE: _____

1. _____
2. _____
3. _____
4. _____
5. _____

DATE: _____

1. _____
2. _____
3. _____
4. _____
5. _____

Follow Up

NOTES AND THOUGHTS ABOUT THE WEEK:

_____
_____
_____

LIFE BALANCE

	0	2	4	6	8	10
PRODUCTIVITY						
STRESS						
_____						

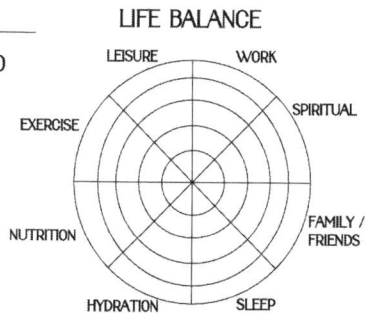

LEISURE · WORK · SPIRITUAL · FAMILY / FRIENDS · SLEEP · HYDRATION · NUTRITION · EXERCISE

INTENTIONAL
Living

4 WEEK ASSESSMENT

CONGRATULATIONS! You have completed a 4-week cycle of your journey toward a more intentional life. Now it's time to take an assessment of that time and effort.

it is important to be honest with yourself and understand that this is a long term commitment, not just a short term goal to meet. Allow yourself some grace to grow and develop good practices, while acknowledging the challenges. Success will come in time and look like a healthier, happier you.

WHAT WENT WELL? _____

_____

_____

_____

WHAT WERE SOME CHALLENGES? _____

_____

_____

_____

_____

WHAT ARE SOME WAYS TO OVERCOME AT LEAST ONE CHALLENGE

GOING FORWARD? _____

_____

_____

_____

DID YOU SEE IMPROVEMENTS IN STRESS LEVELS

AND PRODUCTIVITY? _____

SKETCH / BRAIN DUMP / MOOD BOARD AREA

ANY ADDITIONAL NOTES AND THOUGHTS :

_____
_____
_____
_____

WHERE WILL YOU FOCUS YOUR INTENTIONS DURING

THE NEXT CYCLE? _____

_____
_____

AFFIRMATION OR QUOTE FOR INSPIRATION

KEEP UP THE GOOD WORK

"PRAYER SHOULD BE

THE KEY

OF THE DAY

AND THE LOCK

OF THE NIGHT."

George Herbert

INTENTIONAL
Living

HIGHLIGHT: SPIRITUALITY

This cycle of the Intentional Living Workbook is centered on spirituality. Our connection to a higher power can take many forms. Many participate in an organized religion, while others practice meditation. Some people don't have a defined set of beliefs, but are open to understanding more about how humanity is connected. Whatever form spirituality takes for you, practicing it with intention will deepen your understanding and appreciation.

Intentions surrounding spirituality may be as simple as making attendance at religious services a habit, or by setting aside time each evening to read an affirmation or devotion before meditation or prayer. If you are already doing some of these things, consider expanding spirituality into other aspects of your life. Reflecting a spiritual mindset toward others through your interactions can reduce conflict and stress. Approach relationships through the lens of what humanity has in common, rather than what divides.

Continue to add some spiritual intentions into this cycle, but remember to strive for an overall balance. Check the Resource section for some ideas.

HABIT

INTENTIONAL
Living

WEEKLY WORKBOOK

DATE: _____

1. _____
2. _____
3. _____
4. _____
5. _____

DATE: _____

1. _____
2. _____
3. _____
4. _____
5. _____

DATE: _____

1. _____
2. _____
3. _____
4. _____
5. _____

DATE: _____

1. _____
2. _____
3. _____
4. _____
5. _____

DATE: _____

1. _____
2. _____
3. _____
4. _____
5. _____

DATE: _____

1. _____
2. _____
3. _____
4. _____
5. _____

DATE: _____

1. _____
2. _____
3. _____
4. _____
5. _____

Follow Up

NOTES AND THOUGHTS ABOUT THE WEEK:

_____
_____
_____

LIFE BALANCE

	0	2	4	6	8	10
PRODUCTIVITY						
STRESS						
_____						

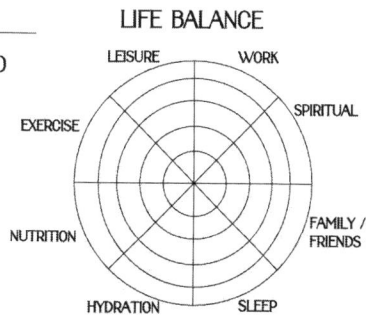

LEISURE   WORK
EXERCISE   SPIRITUAL
NUTRITION   FAMILY / FRIENDS
HYDRATION   SLEEP

INTENTIONAL
Living

WEEKLY WORKBOOK

DATE: _____

1. _____
2. _____
3. _____
4. _____
5. _____

DATE: _____

1. _____
2. _____
3. _____
4. _____
5. _____

DATE: _____

1. _____
2. _____
3. _____
4. _____
5. _____

DATE: _____

1. _____
2. _____
3. _____
4. _____
5. _____

DATE: _____

1. _____
2. _____
3. _____
4. _____
5. _____

DATE: _____

1. _____
2. _____
3. _____
4. _____
5. _____

DATE: _____

1. _____
2. _____
3. _____
4. _____
5. _____

Follow Up

NOTES AND THOUGHTS ABOUT THE WEEK:

_____
_____
_____

LIFE BALANCE

	0	2	4	6	8	10
PRODUCTIVITY						
STRESS						
_____						

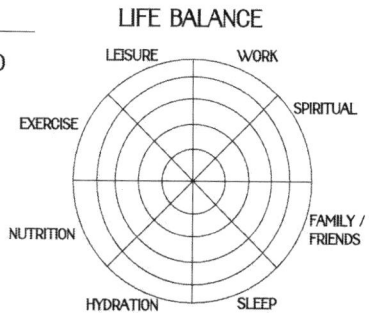

LEISURE   WORK
EXERCISE   SPIRITUAL
NUTRITION   FAMILY / FRIENDS
HYDRATION   SLEEP

INTENTIONAL
Living

WEEKLY WORKBOOK

DATE: _____

1. _____
2. _____
3. _____
4. _____
5. _____

DATE: _____

1. _____
2. _____
3. _____
4. _____
5. _____

DATE: _____

1. _____
2. _____
3. _____
4. _____
5. _____

DATE: _____

1. _____
2. _____
3. _____
4. _____
5. _____

DATE: _____

1. _____
2. _____
3. _____
4. _____
5. _____

DATE: _____

1. _____
2. _____
3. _____
4. _____
5. _____

DATE: _____

1. _____
2. _____
3. _____
4. _____
5. _____

Follow Up

NOTES AND THOUGHTS ABOUT THE WEEK:

_____
_____
_____

LIFE BALANCE

	0	2	4	6	8	10
PRODUCTIVITY						
STRESS						
_____						

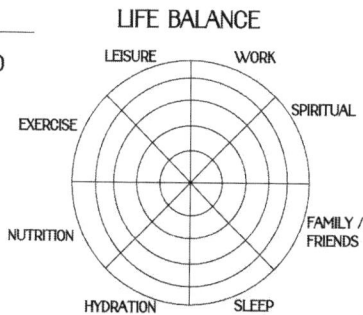

LEISURE   WORK
EXERCISE   SPIRITUAL
NUTRITION   FAMILY / FRIENDS
HYDRATION   SLEEP

INTENTIONAL
Living

WEEKLY WORKBOOK

DATE: _____

1. _____
2. _____
3. _____
4. _____
5. _____

DATE: _____

1. _____
2. _____
3. _____
4. _____
5. _____

DATE: _____

1. _____
2. _____
3. _____
4. _____
5. _____

DATE: _____

1. _____
2. _____
3. _____
4. _____
5. _____

DATE: _____

1. _____
2. _____
3. _____
4. _____
5. _____

DATE: _____

1. _____
2. _____
3. _____
4. _____
5. _____

DATE: _____

1. _____
2. _____
3. _____
4. _____
5. _____

Follow Up

NOTES AND THOUGHTS ABOUT THE WEEK:

_____
_____
_____

LIFE BALANCE

	0	2	4	6	8	10
PRODUCTIVITY						
STRESS						
_____						

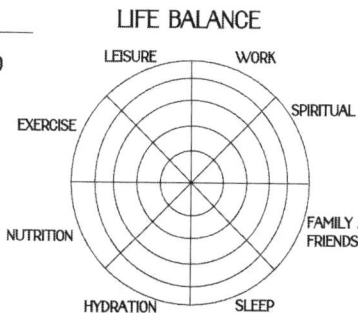

LEISURE WORK
EXERCISE SPIRITUAL
NUTRITION FAMILY / FRIENDS
HYDRATION SLEEP

INTENTIONAL
Living

4 WEEK ASSESSMENT

CONGRATULATIONS! You have completed a 4-week cycle of your journey toward a more intentional life. Now it's time to take an assessment of that time and effort.

it is important to be honest with yourself and understand that this is a long term commitment, not just a short term goal to meet. Allow yourself some grace to grow and develop good practices, while acknowledging the challenges. Success will come in time and look like a healthier, happier you.

WHAT WENT WELL? _____

_____

_____

_____

WHAT WERE SOME CHALLENGES? _____

_____

_____

_____

WHAT ARE SOME WAYS TO OVERCOME AT LEAST ONE CHALLENGE

GOING FORWARD? _____

_____

_____

_____

DID YOU SEE IMPROVEMENTS IN STRESS LEVELS

AND PRODUCTIVITY? _____

SKETCH / BRAIN DUMP / MOOD BOARD AREA

ANY ADDITIONAL NOTES AND THOUGHTS :

_____

_____

_____

_____

WHERE WILL YOU FOCUS YOUR INTENTIONS DURING

THE NEXT CYCLE? _____

_____

_____

AFFIRMATION OR QUOTE FOR INSPIRATION

KEEP UP THE GOOD WORK

"THE ONLY WAY

TO ENJOY ANYTHING

IN LIFE

IS TO EARN IT FIRST."

- Ginger Rogers

INTENTIONAL
Living

HIGHLIGHT: WORK

Work can take many forms, but for purposes of this workbook, work is considered to be your career, or at least the job you do to pay the bills, if you work outside the home. If you are already retired or do not work outside the home, consider this cycle's highlight as a focus on the day-to-day errands and activities you must complete to run your household. Being purposeful in relation to work may not make your dream job appear or manifest unexpected wealth, but it will help you find clarity and hopefully lead to a fulfilling experience.

Work consumes many of our waking hours, so it is important to treat that time with intention, rather than just run on autopilot until the tasks are complete. The only thing we cannot produce more of in life is the invaluable resource of time. Practicing mindfulness with your time and energy while you work will allow you to reclaim precious minutes out of the day and reduce stress.

Making lists to organize the day, speaking with kindness to co-workers or people you encounter, and breaking large tasks into manageable action steps are all ways to bring intention into your work.

HABIT

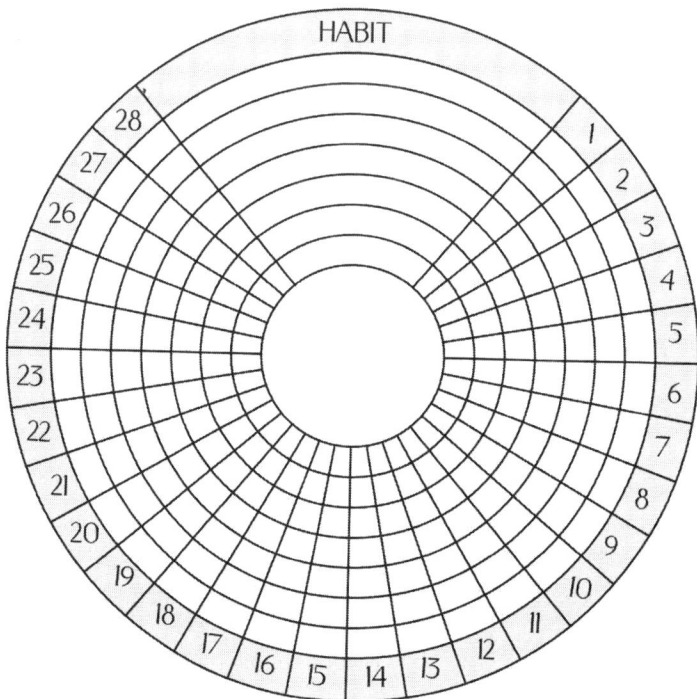

INTENTIONAL
Living

WEEKLY WORKBOOK

DATE: _____

1. _____
2. _____
3. _____
4. _____
5. _____

DATE: _____

1. _____
2. _____
3. _____
4. _____
5. _____

DATE: _____

1. _____
2. _____
3. _____
4. _____
5. _____

DATE: _____

1. _____
2. _____
3. _____
4. _____
5. _____

DATE: _____

1. _____
2. _____
3. _____
4. _____
5. _____

DATE: _____

1. _____
2. _____
3. _____
4. _____
5. _____

DATE: _____

1. _____
2. _____
3. _____
4. _____
5. _____

Follow Up

NOTES AND THOUGHTS ABOUT THE WEEK:

_____

_____

_____

LIFE BALANCE

	0	2	4	6	8	10
PRODUCTIVITY						
STRESS						
_____						

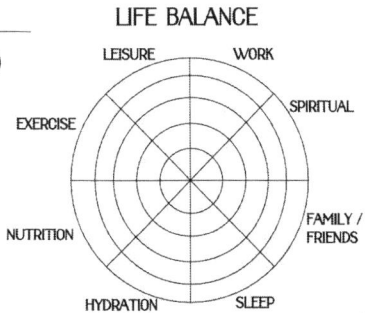

LEISURE — WORK — SPIRITUAL — FAMILY / FRIENDS — SLEEP — HYDRATION — NUTRITION — EXERCISE

INTENTIONAL
Living

WEEKLY WORKBOOK

DATE: _____

1. _____
2. _____
3. _____
4. _____
5. _____

DATE: _____

1. _____
2. _____
3. _____
4. _____
5. _____

DATE: _____

1. _____
2. _____
3. _____
4. _____
5. _____

DATE: _____

1. _____
2. _____
3. _____
4. _____
5. _____

DATE: _____

1. _____
2. _____
3. _____
4. _____
5. _____

DATE: _____

1. _____
2. _____
3. _____
4. _____
5. _____

DATE: _____

1. _____
2. _____
3. _____
4. _____
5. _____

Follow Up

NOTES AND THOUGHTS ABOUT THE WEEK:

_____
_____
_____

LIFE BALANCE

	0	2	4	6	8	10
PRODUCTIVITY						
STRESS						
_____						

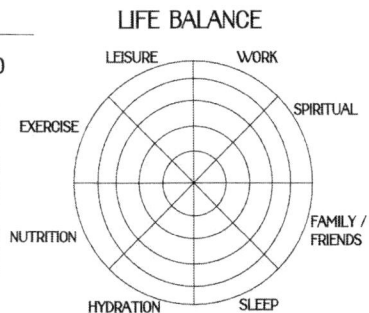

LEISURE   WORK
EXERCISE   SPIRITUAL
NUTRITION   FAMILY / FRIENDS
HYDRATION   SLEEP

INTENTIONAL
Living

WEEKLY WORKBOOK

DATE: _____

1. _____
2. _____
3. _____
4. _____
5. _____

DATE: _____

1. _____
2. _____
3. _____
4. _____
5. _____

DATE: _____

1. _____
2. _____
3. _____
4. _____
5. _____

DATE: _____

1. _____
2. _____
3. _____
4. _____
5. _____

DATE: _____

1. _____
2. _____
3. _____
4. _____
5. _____

DATE: _____

1. _____
2. _____
3. _____
4. _____
5. _____

DATE: _____

1. _____
2. _____
3. _____
4. _____
5. _____

Follow Up

NOTES AND THOUGHTS ABOUT THE WEEK:

_____
_____
_____

LIFE BALANCE

	0	2	4	6	8	10
PRODUCTIVITY						
STRESS						
_____						

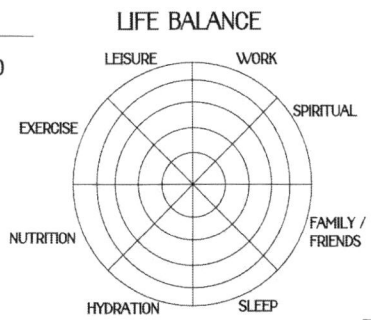

LEISURE · WORK · SPIRITUAL · FAMILY / FRIENDS · SLEEP · HYDRATION · NUTRITION · EXERCISE

INTENTIONAL
Living

WEEKLY WORKBOOK

DATE: _____

1. _____
2. _____
3. _____
4. _____
5. _____

DATE: _____

1. _____
2. _____
3. _____
4. _____
5. _____

DATE: _____

1. _____
2. _____
3. _____
4. _____
5. _____

DATE: _____

1. _____
2. _____
3. _____
4. _____
5. _____

DATE: _____

1. _____
2. _____
3. _____
4. _____
5. _____

DATE: _____

1. _____
2. _____
3. _____
4. _____
5. _____

DATE: _____

1. _____
2. _____
3. _____
4. _____
5. _____

Follow Up

NOTES AND THOUGHTS ABOUT THE WEEK:

_____

_____

_____

LIFE BALANCE

	0	2	4	6	8	10
PRODUCTIVITY						
STRESS						
_____						

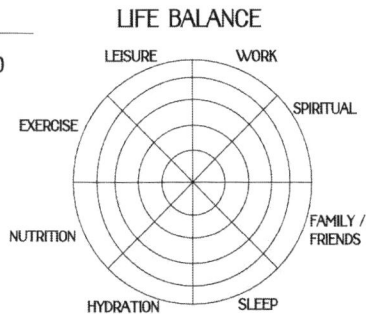

LEISURE WORK
EXERCISE SPIRITUAL
NUTRITION FAMILY / FRIENDS
HYDRATION SLEEP

INTENTIONAL
living

4 WEEK ASSESSMENT

CONGRATULATIONS! You have completed a 4-week cycle of your journey toward a more intentional life. Now it's time to take an assessment of that time and effort.

it is important to be honest with yourself and understand that this is a long term commitment, not just a short term goal to meet. Allow yourself some grace to grow and develop good practices, while acknowledging the challenges. Success will come in time and look like a healthier, happier you.

WHAT WENT WELL? _____

_____

_____

_____

WHAT WERE SOME CHALLENGES? _____

_____

_____

_____

_____

WHAT ARE SOME WAYS TO OVERCOME AT LEAST ONE CHALLENGE

GOING FORWARD? _____

_____

_____

_____

DID YOU SEE IMPROVEMENTS IN STRESS LEVELS

AND PRODUCTIVITY? _____

_____

SKETCH / BRAIN DUMP / MOOD BOARD AREA

ANY ADDITIONAL NOTES AND THOUGHTS :

_____
_____
_____
_____

WHERE WILL YOU FOCUS YOUR INTENTIONS DURING

THE NEXT CYCLE? _____

_____
_____

AFFIRMATION OR QUOTE FOR INSPIRATION

KEEP UP THE GOOD WORK

"WHEN YOU TAKE TIME TO
REPLENISH YOUR SPIRIT,
IT ALLOWS YOU TO SERVE
OTHERS FROM THE
OVERFLOW.
YOU CANNOT SERVE FROM
AN EMPTY VESSEL"

- Elenor Brownn

INTENTIONAL
Living

HIGHLIGHT: LEISURE / SELF CARE

Life is not truly balanced if there is no time for leisure and self-care. Spending time with family and friends, sleep and spirituality are all restorative to your soul, but taking some time for yourself is equally important. It is sometimes far too easy to get into routines where you put yourself last, if at all, in all life's busy moments. Building leisure and self-care intentions into your daily life intention lists will bring those ideas front and center, making them harder to push aside.

In this 4 week cycle, it is time to find some ways to focus on yourself. These can be simple gestures, like making yourself a cup of tea to sip in the fresh morning air, or beginning more involved undertakings like learning a new language or craft. Be sure this is separate from activities you do with others - this is "me" time.

Sometimes self-care can also mean setting boundaries. Allow yourself to write some intentions that involve saying no with kindness. Give yourself permission to eliminate things or habits in your life that are using up your energy or time in a negative way. Mindfulness isn't always about adding...subtracting is important, too.

HABIT

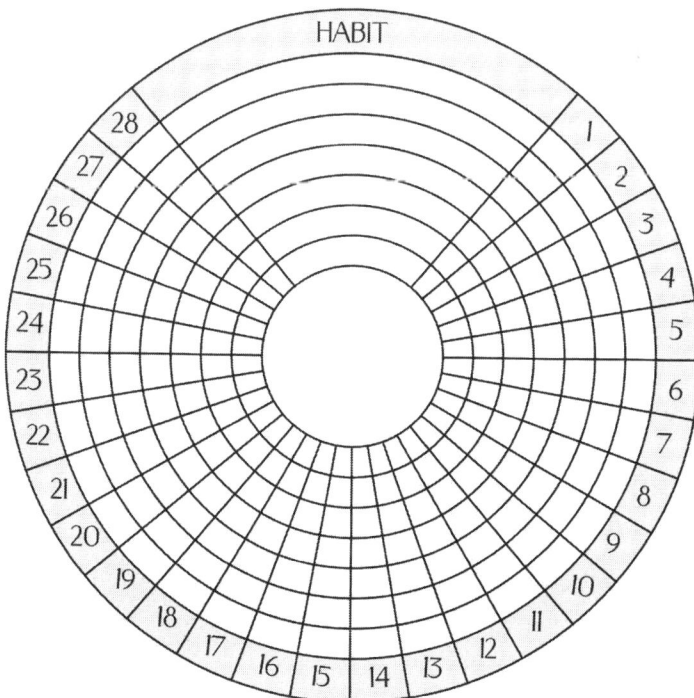

INTENTIONAL
Living

WEEKLY WORKBOOK

DATE: _____

1. _____
2. _____
3. _____
4. _____
5. _____

DATE: _____

1. _____
2. _____
3. _____
4. _____
5. _____

DATE: _____

1. _____
2. _____
3. _____
4. _____
5. _____

DATE: _____

1. _____
2. _____
3. _____
4. _____
5. _____

DATE: _____

1. _____
2. _____
3. _____
4. _____
5. _____

DATE: _____

1. _____
2. _____
3. _____
4. _____
5. _____

DATE: _____

1. _____
2. _____
3. _____
4. _____
5. _____

Follow Up

NOTES AND THOUGHTS ABOUT THE WEEK:

_____

_____

_____

LIFE BALANCE

	0	2	4	6	8	10
PRODUCTIVITY						
STRESS						
_____						

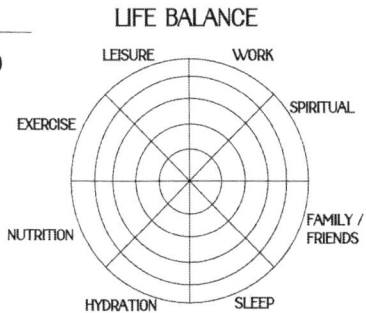

LEISURE · WORK · SPIRITUAL · FAMILY / FRIENDS · SLEEP · HYDRATION · NUTRITION · EXERCISE

INTENTIONAL
Living

WEEKLY WORKBOOK

DATE: _____

1. _____
2. _____
3. _____
4. _____
5. _____

DATE: _____

1. _____
2. _____
3. _____
4. _____
5. _____

DATE: _____

1. _____
2. _____
3. _____
4. _____
5. _____

DATE: _____

1. _____
2. _____
3. _____
4. _____
5. _____

DATE: _____

1. _____
2. _____
3. _____
4. _____
5. _____

DATE: _____

1. _____
2. _____
3. _____
4. _____
5. _____

DATE: _____

1. _____
2. _____
3. _____
4. _____
5. _____

Follow Up

NOTES AND THOUGHTS ABOUT THE WEEK:

_____
_____
_____

LIFE BALANCE

	0	2	4	6	8	10
PRODUCTIVITY						
STRESS						
_____						

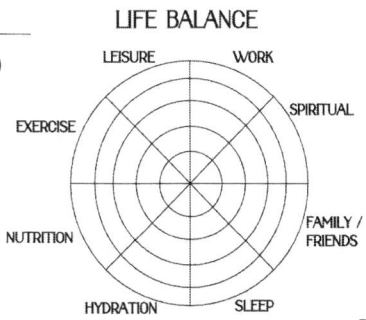

LEISURE WORK SPIRITUAL EXERCISE NUTRITION HYDRATION SLEEP FAMILY / FRIENDS

INTENTIONAL
Living

WEEKLY WORKBOOK

DATE: _____

1. _____
2. _____
3. _____
4. _____
5. _____

DATE: _____

1. _____
2. _____
3. _____
4. _____
5. _____

DATE: _____

1. _____
2. _____
3. _____
4. _____
5. _____

DATE: _____

1. _____
2. _____
3. _____
4. _____
5. _____

DATE: _____

1. _____
2. _____
3. _____
4. _____
5. _____

DATE: _____

1. _____
2. _____
3. _____
4. _____
5. _____

DATE: _____

1. _____
2. _____
3. _____
4. _____
5. _____

Follow Up

NOTES AND THOUGHTS ABOUT THE WEEK:

_____
_____
_____

LIFE BALANCE

	0	2	4	6	8	10
PRODUCTIVITY						
STRESS						
_____						

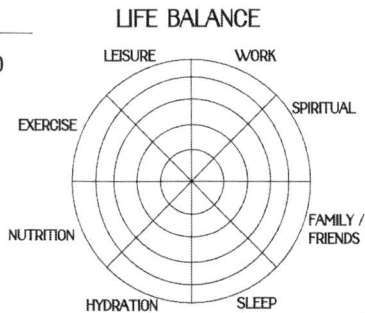

LEISURE   WORK
EXERCISE   SPIRITUAL
NUTRITION   FAMILY / FRIENDS
HYDRATION   SLEEP

INTENTIONAL
Living

WEEKLY WORKBOOK

DATE: _____

1. _____
2. _____
3. _____
4. _____
5. _____

DATE: _____

1. _____
2. _____
3. _____
4. _____
5. _____

DATE: _____

1. _____
2. _____
3. _____
4. _____
5. _____

DATE: _____

1. _____
2. _____
3. _____
4. _____
5. _____

DATE: _____

1. _____
2. _____
3. _____
4. _____
5. _____

DATE: _____

1. _____
2. _____
3. _____
4. _____
5. _____

DATE: _____

1. _____
2. _____
3. _____
4. _____
5. _____

Follow Up

NOTES AND THOUGHTS ABOUT THE WEEK:

_____

_____

_____

LIFE BALANCE

	0	2	4	6	8	10
PRODUCTIVITY						
STRESS						
_____						

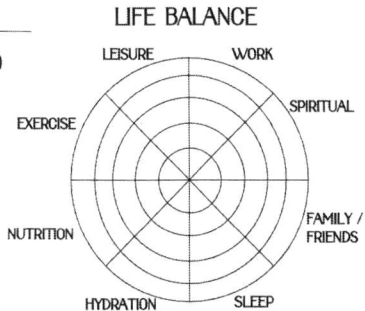

LEISURE — WORK — SPIRITUAL — FAMILY / FRIENDS — SLEEP — HYDRATION — NUTRITION — EXERCISE

INTENTIONAL
living

4 WEEK ASSESSMENT

CONGRATULATIONS! You have completed a 4-week cycle of your journey toward a more intentional life. Now it's time to take an assessment of that time and effort.

it is important to be honest with yourself and understand that this is a long term commitment, not just a short term goal to meet. Allow yourself some grace to grow and develop good practices, while acknowledging the challenges. Success will come in time and look like a healthier, happier you.

WHAT WENT WELL? _____

_____

_____

_____

WHAT WERE SOME CHALLENGES? _____

_____

_____

_____

_____

WHAT ARE SOME WAYS TO OVERCOME AT LEAST ONE CHALLENGE

GOING FORWARD? _____

_____

_____

_____

DID YOU SEE IMPROVEMENTS IN STRESS LEVELS

AND PRODUCTIVITY? _____

_____

SKETCH / BRAIN DUMP / MOOD BOARD AREA

ANY ADDITIONAL NOTES AND THOUGHTS :

_____

_____

_____

_____

WHERE WILL YOU FOCUS YOUR INTENTIONS DURING

THE NEXT CYCLE? _____

_____

_____

AFFIRMATION OR QUOTE FOR INSPIRATION

KEEP UP THE GOOD WORK

"IT IS HEALTH
THAT IS REAL
WEALTH,
AND NOT PIECES
OF
GOLD AND SILVER."

- Mahatma Gandhi

INTENTIONAL
Living

HIGHLIGHT: EXERCISE

While the last few highlights have gone into depth about maintaining balance of the mind and soul, the final wellness areas are going to deal with the health of the physical body.

This tenth cycle centers around exercise. It's one of the most important factors in maintaining overall health, however, for many, it's one of the most difficult areas in which to introduce intention and mindfulness. It is so often just easier to put off daily exercise in favor of something else during the day that has to be done. If this sounds familiar, plan to start with manageable action steps in the daily intention workbook or a small goal in the habit section to jump start the process.

If exercise is already part of your daily routine, that is wonderful! You don't have to expand your intentions by buying expensive equipment or memberships, but do look for other ways to add mindfulness. Seek out exercise activities that also benefit charities, offer to join a friend for a walk/hike/run, or even sponsor a child who has an interest in a sport or activity, but who cannot afford the equipment or fees.

HABIT

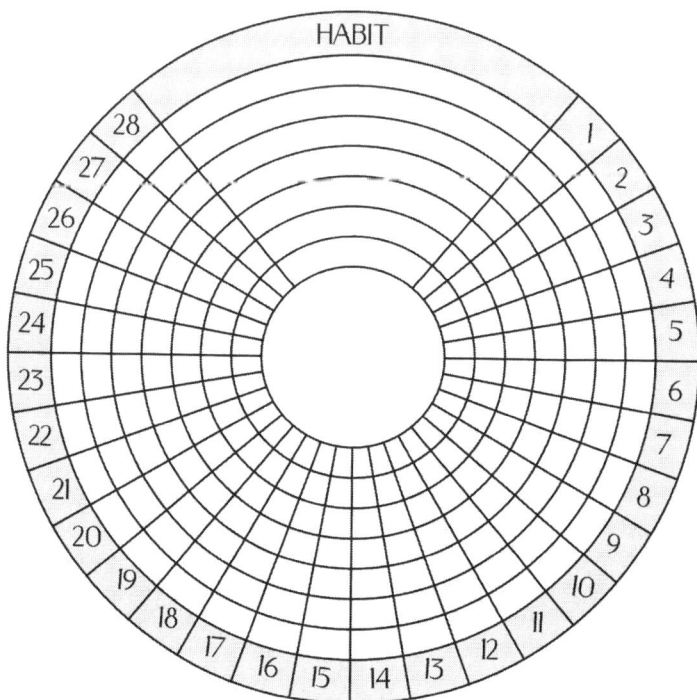

INTENTIONAL
Living

WEEKLY WORKBOOK

DATE: _____

1. _____
2. _____
3. _____
4. _____
5. _____

DATE: _____

1. _____
2. _____
3. _____
4. _____
5. _____

DATE: _____

1. _____
2. _____
3. _____
4. _____
5. _____

DATE: _____

1. _____
2. _____
3. _____
4. _____
5. _____

DATE: _____

1. _____
2. _____
3. _____
4. _____
5. _____

DATE: _____

1. _____
2. _____
3. _____
4. _____
5. _____

DATE: _____

1. _____
2. _____
3. _____
4. _____
5. _____

Follow Up

NOTES AND THOUGHTS ABOUT THE WEEK:

_____
_____
_____

LIFE BALANCE

	0	2	4	6	8	10
PRODUCTIVITY						
STRESS						
_____						

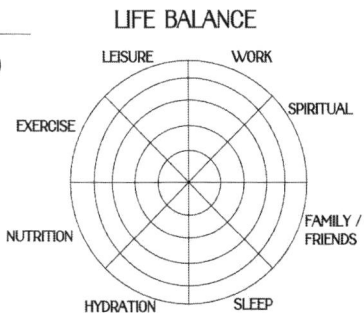

LEISURE WORK
EXERCISE SPIRITUAL
NUTRITION FAMILY / FRIENDS
HYDRATION SLEEP

INTENTIONAL
Living

WEEKLY WORKBOOK

DATE: _____

1. _____
2. _____
3. _____
4. _____
5. _____

DATE: _____

1. _____
2. _____
3. _____
4. _____
5. _____

DATE: _____

1. _____
2. _____
3. _____
4. _____
5. _____

DATE: _____

1. _____
2. _____
3. _____
4. _____
5. _____

DATE: _____

1. _____
2. _____
3. _____
4. _____
5. _____

DATE: _____

1. _____
2. _____
3. _____
4. _____
5. _____

DATE: _____

1. _____
2. _____
3. _____
4. _____
5. _____

Follow Up

NOTES AND THOUGHTS ABOUT THE WEEK:

_____
_____
_____

LIFE BALANCE

	0	2	4	6	8	10
PRODUCTIVITY						
STRESS						
_____						

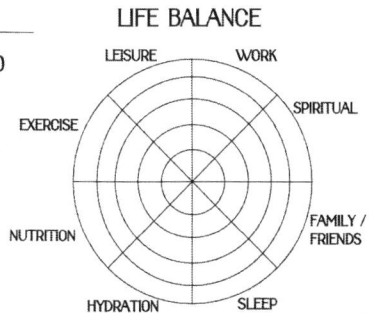

LEISURE — WORK — SPIRITUAL — FAMILY / FRIENDS — SLEEP — HYDRATION — NUTRITION — EXERCISE

INTENTIONAL
Living

WEEKLY WORKBOOK

DATE: _____

1. _____
2. _____
3. _____
4. _____
5. _____

DATE: _____

1. _____
2. _____
3. _____
4. _____
5. _____

DATE: _____

1. _____
2. _____
3. _____
4. _____
5. _____

DATE: _____

1. _____
2. _____
3. _____
4. _____
5. _____

DATE: _____

1. _____
2. _____
3. _____
4. _____
5. _____

DATE: _____

1. _____
2. _____
3. _____
4. _____
5. _____

DATE: _____

1. _____
2. _____
3. _____
4. _____
5. _____

Follow Up

NOTES AND THOUGHTS ABOUT THE WEEK:

_____
_____
_____

LIFE BALANCE

	0	2	4	6	8	10
PRODUCTIVITY						
STRESS						
_____						

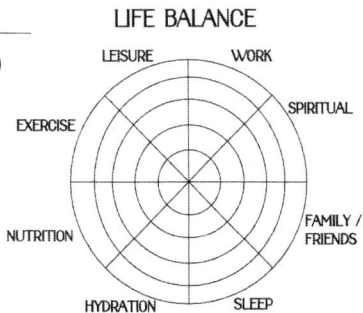

LEISURE · WORK · SPIRITUAL · FAMILY / FRIENDS · SLEEP · HYDRATION · NUTRITION · EXERCISE

INTENTIONAL
Living

WEEKLY WORKBOOK

DATE: _____

1. _____
2. _____
3. _____
4. _____
5. _____

DATE: _____

1. _____
2. _____
3. _____
4. _____
5. _____

DATE: _____

1. _____
2. _____
3. _____
4. _____
5. _____

DATE: _____

1. _____
2. _____
3. _____
4. _____
5. _____

DATE: _____

1. _____
2. _____
3. _____
4. _____
5. _____

DATE: _____

1. _____
2. _____
3. _____
4. _____
5. _____

DATE: _____

1. _____
2. _____
3. _____
4. _____
5. _____

Follow Up

NOTES AND THOUGHTS ABOUT THE WEEK:

_____

_____

_____

LIFE BALANCE

	0	2	4	6	8	10
PRODUCTIVITY						
STRESS						
_____						

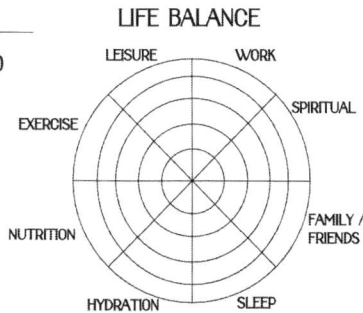

LEISURE WORK
EXERCISE SPIRITUAL
NUTRITION FAMILY / FRIENDS
HYDRATION SLEEP

INTENTIONAL
Living

4 WEEK ASSESSMENT

CONGRATULATIONS! You have completed a 4-week cycle of your journey toward a more intentional life. Now it's time to take an assessment of that time and effort.

it is important to be honest with yourself and understand that this is a long term commitment, not just a short term goal to meet. Allow yourself some grace to grow and develop good practices, while acknowledging the challenges. Success will come in time and look like a healthier, happier you.

WHAT WENT WELL? _____

_____

_____

_____

WHAT WERE SOME CHALLENGES? _____

_____

_____

_____

_____

WHAT ARE SOME WAYS TO OVERCOME AT LEAST ONE CHALLENGE

GOING FORWARD? _____

_____

_____

_____

DID YOU SEE IMPROVEMENTS IN STRESS LEVELS

AND PRODUCTIVITY? _____

SKETCH / BRAIN DUMP / MOOD BOARD AREA

ANY ADDITIONAL NOTES AND THOUGHTS :

_____

_____

_____

_____

WHERE WILL YOU FOCUS YOUR INTENTIONS DURING

THE NEXT CYCLE? _____

_____

_____

AFFIRMATION OR QUOTE FOR INSPIRATION

KEEP UP THE GOOD WORK

"OUR GREATEST GLORY

IS NOT IN

NEVER FAILING,

BUT IN RISING

EVERY TIME WE FALL"

- Confucius

INTENTIONAL
Living

HIGHLIGHT: NUTRITION

In this cycle, we highlight how to develop intention with the food we consume. There are many ways to be purposeful with nutrition, even though sometimes it is not the easiest task. Keeping moderation and balance in mind, seek out ways over the next few weeks to bring intention to your food choices.

There may be some days or spans of time where intentionality is seen in some of the foundational ways. Eating three healthy meals during the day, add one fresh fruit and vegetable per day, or avoiding sugary sweets can all be ways to add purpose to nutrition, without pushing too many changes all at once. Aim for small successes at first.

If you have expanded beyond nutritional basics, add mindfulness by trying new recipes, planting your own garden, or even adding some healthy items to your grocery cart for donation to your local food bank or other charity.

As always, consult your health care professional with questions or concerns before starting any exercise or diet-related lifestyle change.

HABIT

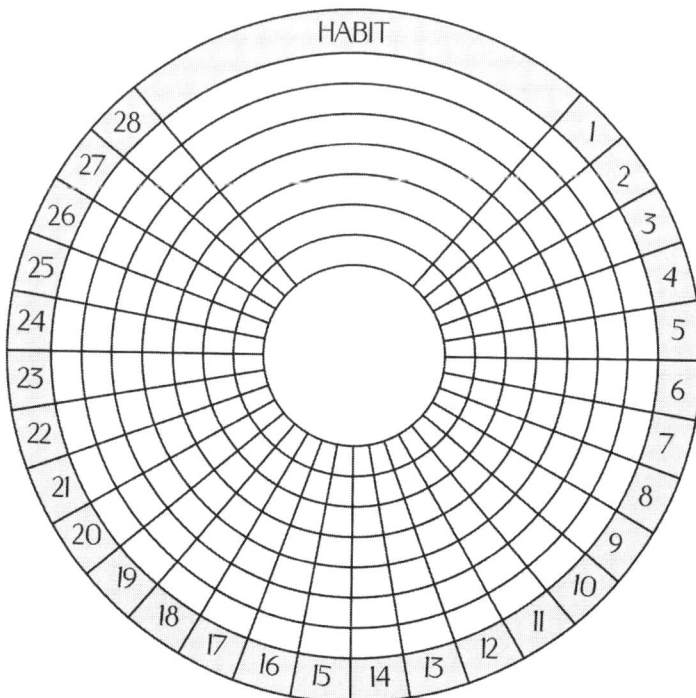

INTENTIONAL
Living

WEEKLY WORKBOOK

DATE: _____

1. _____
2. _____
3. _____
4. _____
5. _____

DATE: _____

1. _____
2. _____
3. _____
4. _____
5. _____

DATE: _____

1. _____
2. _____
3. _____
4. _____
5. _____

DATE: _____

1. _____
2. _____
3. _____
4. _____
5. _____

DATE: _____

1. _____
2. _____
3. _____
4. _____
5. _____

DATE: _____

1. _____
2. _____
3. _____
4. _____
5. _____

DATE: _____

1. _____
2. _____
3. _____
4. _____
5. _____

Follow Up

NOTES AND THOUGHTS ABOUT THE WEEK:

_____
_____
_____

LIFE BALANCE

	0	2	4	6	8	10
PRODUCTIVITY						
STRESS						
_____						

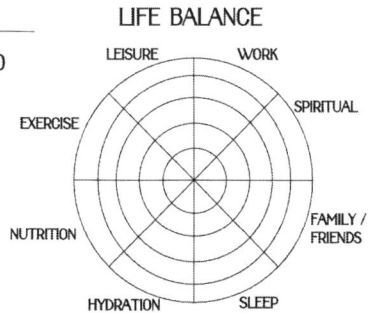

LEISURE WORK
EXERCISE SPIRITUAL
NUTRITION FAMILY / FRIENDS
HYDRATION SLEEP

INTENTIONAL
Living

WEEKLY WORKBOOK

DATE: _____

1. _____
2. _____
3. _____
4. _____
5. _____

DATE: _____

1. _____
2. _____
3. _____
4. _____
5. _____

DATE: _____

1. _____
2. _____
3. _____
4. _____
5. _____

DATE: _____

1. _____
2. _____
3. _____
4. _____
5. _____

DATE: _____

1. _____
2. _____
3. _____
4. _____
5. _____

DATE: _____

1. _____
2. _____
3. _____
4. _____
5. _____

DATE: _____

1. _____
2. _____
3. _____
4. _____
5. _____

Follow Up

NOTES AND THOUGHTS ABOUT THE WEEK:

_____

_____

_____

LIFE BALANCE

	0	2	4	6	8	10
PRODUCTIVITY						
STRESS						
_____						

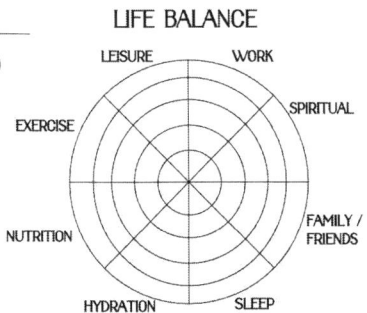

LEISURE WORK SPIRITUAL EXERCISE FAMILY / FRIENDS NUTRITION SLEEP HYDRATION

INTENTIONAL
Living

WEEKLY WORKBOOK

DATE: _____

1. _____
2. _____
3. _____
4. _____
5. _____

DATE: _____

1. _____
2. _____
3. _____
4. _____
5. _____

DATE: _____

1. _____
2. _____
3. _____
4. _____
5. _____

DATE: _____

1. _____
2. _____
3. _____
4. _____
5. _____

DATE: _____

1. _____
2. _____
3. _____
4. _____
5. _____

DATE: _____

1. _____
2. _____
3. _____
4. _____
5. _____

DATE: _____

1. _____
2. _____
3. _____
4. _____
5. _____

Follow Up

NOTES AND THOUGHTS ABOUT THE WEEK:

_____
_____
_____

	0	2	4	6	8	10
PRODUCTIVITY						
STRESS						
_____						

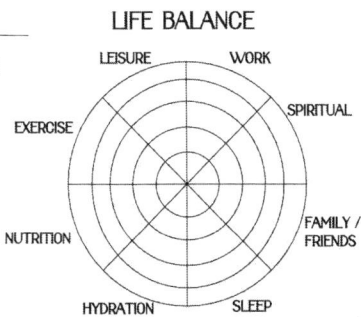

LIFE BALANCE

LEISURE WORK SPIRITUAL EXERCISE FAMILY / FRIENDS NUTRITION HYDRATION SLEEP

INTENTIONAL
Living

WEEKLY WORKBOOK

DATE: _____

1. _____
2. _____
3. _____
4. _____
5. _____

DATE: _____

1. _____
2. _____
3. _____
4. _____
5. _____

DATE: _____

1. _____
2. _____
3. _____
4. _____
5. _____

DATE: _____

1. _____
2. _____
3. _____
4. _____
5. _____

DATE: _____

1. _____
2. _____
3. _____
4. _____
5. _____

DATE: _____

1. _____
2. _____
3. _____
4. _____
5. _____

DATE: _____

1. _____
2. _____
3. _____
4. _____
5. _____

Follow Up

NOTES AND THOUGHTS ABOUT THE WEEK:

_____

_____

_____

	0	2	4	6	8	10
PRODUCTIVITY						
STRESS						

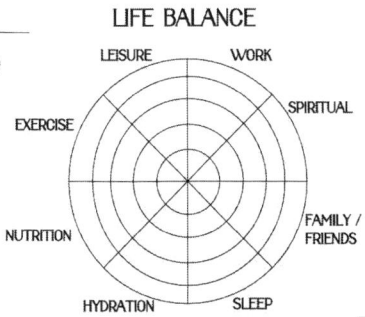

LIFE BALANCE

LEISURE WORK

EXERCISE SPIRITUAL

NUTRITION FAMILY / FRIENDS

HYDRATION SLEEP

INTENTIONAL
Living

4 WEEK ASSESSMENT

CONGRATULATIONS! You have completed a 4-week cycle of your journey toward a more intentional life. Now it's time to take an assessment of that time and effort.

it is important to be honest with yourself and understand that this is a long term commitment, not just a short term goal to meet. Allow yourself some grace to grow and develop good practices, while acknowledging the challenges. Success will come in time and look like a healthier, happier you.

WHAT WENT WELL? _____

_____

_____

_____

WHAT WERE SOME CHALLENGES? _____

_____

_____

_____

_____

WHAT ARE SOME WAYS TO OVERCOME AT LEAST ONE CHALLENGE

GOING FORWARD? _____

_____

_____

_____

DID YOU SEE IMPROVEMENTS IN STRESS LEVELS

AND PRODUCTIVITY? _____

SKETCH / BRAIN DUMP / MOOD BOARD AREA

ANY ADDITIONAL NOTES AND THOUGHTS :

_____

_____

_____

_____

WHERE WILL YOU FOCUS YOUR INTENTIONS DURING

THE NEXT CYCLE? _____

_____

_____

AFFIRMATION OR QUOTE FOR INSPIRATION

KEEP UP THE GOOD WORK

"LIFE CAN ONLY BE
UNDERSTOOD
BACKWARDS,
BUT IT MUST BE
LIVED FORWARDS."

- Soren Kierkegaard

INTENTIONAL
Living

HIGHLIGHT: HYDRATION

Welcome to the 12th cycle of your Intentional Living year! This highlight's focus is on the importance of good hydration to your overall health. It may not seem that there is a great need to add intentionality to staying hydrated throughout the day, but if you have ever experienced any of the issues associated with being dehydrated, you know that mindfulness in this area can prevent a lot of problems.

For some, it may be as easy as adding a reminder on the habit tracker or using a line on the weekly workbook to succeed at staying hydrated. For others who find that challenging, plan a gradual increase in your daily intentional workbook up to a comfortable level that can be maintained with success. Then, expand those steps up to the desired level for long-term health benefits. Take the time you need.

When you are ready to add an additional level of mindfulness to the concept of hydration, consider sponsoring programs that provide clean water to drought-stricken or polluted areas around the world. Access to clean water and adequate hydration is important for everyone.

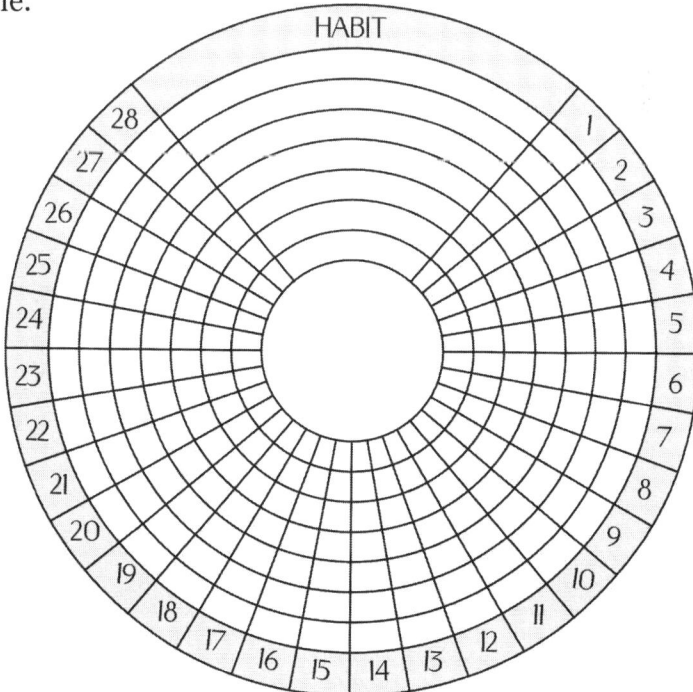

HABIT

1 2 3 4 5 6 7 8 9 10 11 12 13 14 15 16 17 18 19 20 21 22 23 24 25 26 27 28

INTENTIONAL
Living

WEEKLY WORKBOOK

DATE: _____

1. _____
2. _____
3. _____
4. _____
5. _____

DATE: _____

1. _____
2. _____
3. _____
4. _____
5. _____

DATE: _____

1. _____
2. _____
3. _____
4. _____
5. _____

DATE: _____

1. _____
2. _____
3. _____
4. _____
5. _____

DATE: _____

1. _____
2. _____
3. _____
4. _____
5. _____

DATE: _____

1. _____
2. _____
3. _____
4. _____
5. _____

DATE: _____

1. _____
2. _____
3. _____
4. _____
5. _____

Follow Up

NOTES AND THOUGHTS ABOUT THE WEEK:

_____
_____
_____

LIFE BALANCE

	0	2	4	6	8	10
PRODUCTIVITY						
STRESS						
_____						

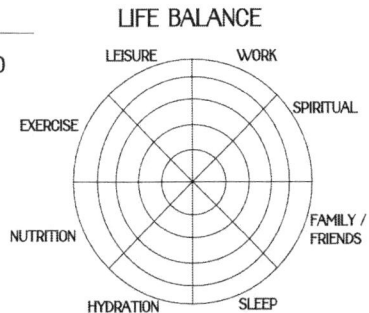

LEISURE WORK
EXERCISE SPIRITUAL
NUTRITION FAMILY / FRIENDS
HYDRATION SLEEP

INTENTIONAL
Living

WEEKLY WORKBOOK

DATE: _____

1. _____
2. _____
3. _____
4. _____
5. _____

DATE: _____

1. _____
2. _____
3. _____
4. _____
5. _____

DATE: _____

1. _____
2. _____
3. _____
4. _____
5. _____

DATE: _____

1. _____
2. _____
3. _____
4. _____
5. _____

DATE: _____

1. _____
2. _____
3. _____
4. _____
5. _____

DATE: _____

1. _____
2. _____
3. _____
4. _____
5. _____

DATE: _____

1. _____
2. _____
3. _____
4. _____
5. _____

Follow Up

NOTES AND THOUGHTS ABOUT THE WEEK:

_____

_____

_____

LIFE BALANCE

	0	2	4	6	8	10
PRODUCTIVITY						
STRESS						
_____						

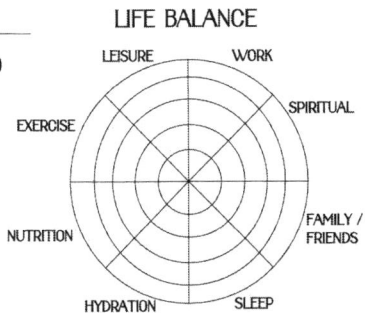

LEISURE · WORK · SPIRITUAL · FAMILY / FRIENDS · SLEEP · HYDRATION · NUTRITION · EXERCISE

INTENTIONAL
Living

WEEKLY WORKBOOK

DATE: _____

1. _____
2. _____
3. _____
4. _____
5. _____

DATE: _____

1. _____
2. _____
3. _____
4. _____
5. _____

DATE: _____

1. _____
2. _____
3. _____
4. _____
5. _____

DATE: _____

1. _____
2. _____
3. _____
4. _____
5. _____

DATE: _____

1. _____
2. _____
3. _____
4. _____
5. _____

DATE: _____

1. _____
2. _____
3. _____
4. _____
5. _____

DATE: _____

1. _____
2. _____
3. _____
4. _____
5. _____

Follow Up

NOTES AND THOUGHTS ABOUT THE WEEK:

_____
_____
_____

LIFE BALANCE

	0	2	4	6	8	10
PRODUCTIVITY						
STRESS						
_____						

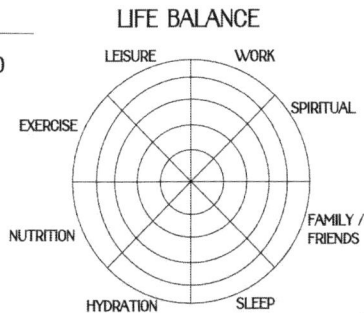

LEISURE   WORK
SPIRITUAL
EXERCISE
FAMILY / FRIENDS
NUTRITION
HYDRATION   SLEEP

INTENTIONAL
Living

WEEKLY WORKBOOK

DATE: _____

1. _____
2. _____
3. _____
4. _____
5. _____

DATE: _____

1. _____
2. _____
3. _____
4. _____
5. _____

DATE: _____

1. _____
2. _____
3. _____
4. _____
5. _____

DATE: _____

1. _____
2. _____
3. _____
4. _____
5. _____

DATE: _____

1. _____
2. _____
3. _____
4. _____
5. _____

DATE: _____

1. _____
2. _____
3. _____
4. _____
5. _____

DATE: _____

1. _____
2. _____
3. _____
4. _____
5. _____

Follow Up

NOTES AND THOUGHTS ABOUT THE WEEK:

_____

_____

_____

LIFE BALANCE

	0	2	4	6	8	10
PRODUCTIVITY						
STRESS						
_____						

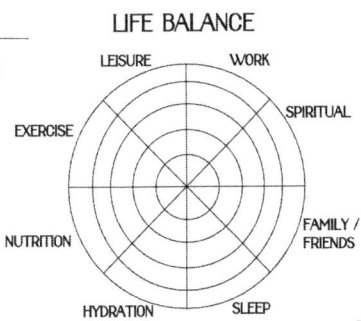

LEISURE   WORK

EXERCISE   SPIRITUAL

NUTRITION   FAMILY / FRIENDS

HYDRATION   SLEEP

INTENTIONAL
living

4 WEEK ASSESSMENT

CONGRATULATIONS! You have completed a 4-week cycle of your journey toward a more intentional life. Now it's time to take an assessment of that time and effort.

it is important to be honest with yourself and understand that this is a long term commitment, not just a short term goal to meet. Allow yourself some grace to grow and develop good practices, while acknowledging the challenges. Success will come in time and look like a healthier, happier you.

WHAT WENT WELL? _____

_____

_____

_____

WHAT WERE SOME CHALLENGES? _____

_____

_____

_____

_____

WHAT ARE SOME WAYS TO OVERCOME AT LEAST ONE CHALLENGE

GOING FORWARD? _____

_____

_____

_____

DID YOU SEE IMPROVEMENTS IN STRESS LEVELS

AND PRODUCTIVITY? _____

SKETCH / BRAIN DUMP / MOOD BOARD AREA

ANY ADDITIONAL NOTES AND THOUGHTS :

_____

_____

_____

_____

WHERE WILL YOU FOCUS YOUR INTENTIONS DURING

THE NEXT CYCLE? _____

_____

_____

AFFIRMATION OR QUOTE FOR INSPIRATION

KEEP UP THE GOOD WORK

"WE CAN DO
ANYTHING
WE WANT TO
IF WE STICK
WITH IT
LONG ENOUGH."

-Helen Keller

INTENTIONAL
Living

HIGHLIGHT: SLEEP

You have come to the final four week cycle of the Intentional Living Workbook! Take a moment to reflect on what an accomplishment this is and how far you've progressed.

This final highlight is about bringing mindfulness to sleep. The restorative hours your body needs every night to rest and repair both the mind and body are so often shorted due to busy schedules, restless minds, or other parts of life demanding more waking hours. This can wear you down over time, and negatively effect so many aspects of your health.

Bring intentionality to your sleep schedule with both actionable steps and longer-term goals. Having a cut-off time for social media at night may be a quick way to help your mind calm down and prepare for sleep. Adjusting your work habits to eliminate late evening projects and emails might take longer to accomplish, but it is a purposeful process that will have benefits in the future.

Check the Resource area for more ideas on how to add purposeful routines and habits.

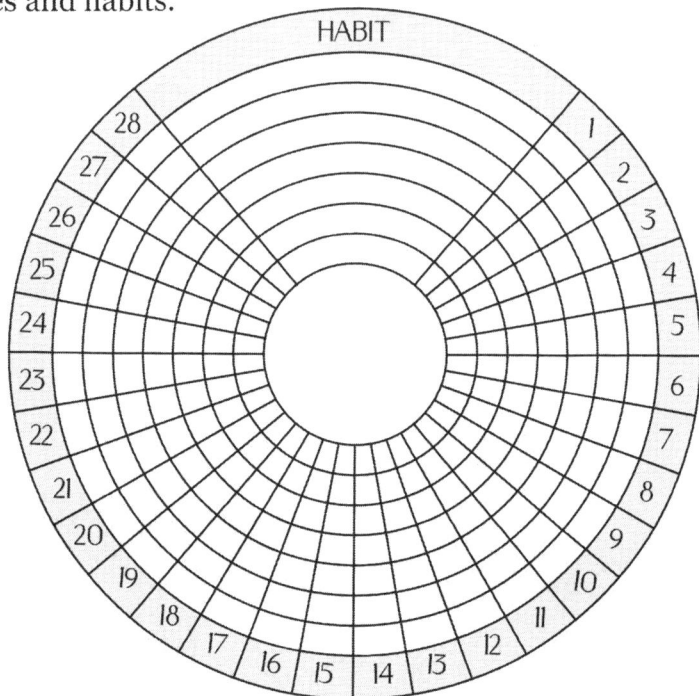

HABIT

28 27 26 25 24 23 22 21 20 19 18 17 16 15 14 13 12 11 10 9 8 7 6 5 4 3 2 1

INTENTIONAL
Living

WEEKLY WORKBOOK

DATE: _____

1. _____
2. _____
3. _____
4. _____
5. _____

DATE: _____

1. _____
2. _____
3. _____
4. _____
5. _____

DATE: _____

1. _____
2. _____
3. _____
4. _____
5. _____

DATE: _____

1. _____
2. _____
3. _____
4. _____
5. _____

DATE: _____

1. _____
2. _____
3. _____
4. _____
5. _____

DATE: _____

1. _____
2. _____
3. _____
4. _____
5. _____

DATE: _____

1. _____
2. _____
3. _____
4. _____
5. _____

Follow Up

NOTES AND THOUGHTS ABOUT THE WEEK:

_____
_____
_____

LIFE BALANCE

	0	2	4	6	8	10
PRODUCTIVITY						
STRESS						
_____						

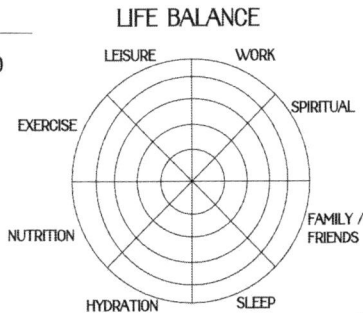

LEISURE · WORK · SPIRITUAL · FAMILY / FRIENDS · SLEEP · HYDRATION · NUTRITION · EXERCISE

INTENTIONAL
Living

WEEKLY WORKBOOK

DATE: _____

1. _____
2. _____
3. _____
4. _____
5. _____

DATE: _____

1. _____
2. _____
3. _____
4. _____
5. _____

DATE: _____

1. _____
2. _____
3. _____
4. _____
5. _____

DATE: _____

1. _____
2. _____
3. _____
4. _____
5. _____

DATE: _____

1. _____
2. _____
3. _____
4. _____
5. _____

DATE: _____

1. _____
2. _____
3. _____
4. _____
5. _____

DATE: _____

1. _____
2. _____
3. _____
4. _____
5. _____

Follow Up

NOTES AND THOUGHTS ABOUT THE WEEK:

_____
_____
_____

LIFE BALANCE

	0	2	4	6	8	10
PRODUCTIVITY						
STRESS						
_____						

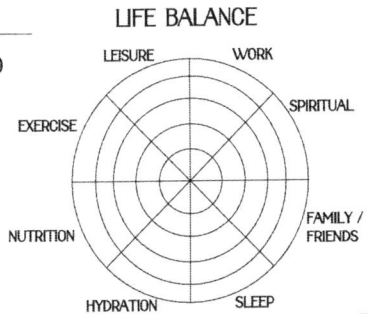

LEISURE   WORK
EXERCISE   SPIRITUAL
NUTRITION   FAMILY / FRIENDS
HYDRATION   SLEEP

INTENTIONAL
Living

WEEKLY WORKBOOK

DATE: _____

1. _____
2. _____
3. _____
4. _____
5. _____

DATE: _____

1. _____
2. _____
3. _____
4. _____
5. _____

DATE: _____

1. _____
2. _____
3. _____
4. _____
5. _____

DATE: _____

1. _____
2. _____
3. _____
4. _____
5. _____

DATE: _____

1. _____
2. _____
3. _____
4. _____
5. _____

DATE: _____

1. _____
2. _____
3. _____
4. _____
5. _____

DATE: _____

1. _____
2. _____
3. _____
4. _____
5. _____

Follow Up

NOTES AND THOUGHTS ABOUT THE WEEK:

_____

_____

_____

LIFE BALANCE

	0	2	4	6	8	10
PRODUCTIVITY						
STRESS						
_____						

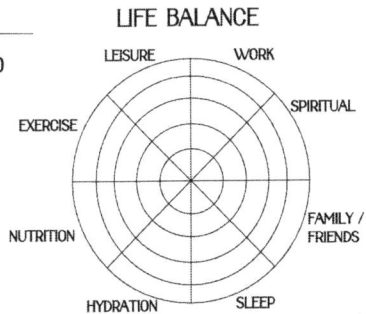

LEISURE   WORK
EXERCISE   SPIRITUAL
NUTRITION   FAMILY / FRIENDS
HYDRATION   SLEEP

INTENTIONAL
Living

WEEKLY WORKBOOK

DATE: _____

1. _____
2. _____
3. _____
4. _____
5. _____

DATE: _____

1. _____
2. _____
3. _____
4. _____
5. _____

DATE: _____

1. _____
2. _____
3. _____
4. _____
5. _____

DATE: _____

1. _____
2. _____
3. _____
4. _____
5. _____

DATE: _____

1. _____
2. _____
3. _____
4. _____
5. _____

DATE: _____

1. _____
2. _____
3. _____
4. _____
5. _____

DATE: _____

1. _____
2. _____
3. _____
4. _____
5. _____

Follow Up

NOTES AND THOUGHTS ABOUT THE WEEK:

_____

_____

_____

	0	2	4	6	8	10
PRODUCTIVITY						
STRESS						

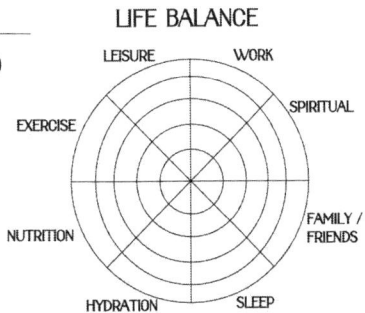

LIFE BALANCE

LEISURE WORK

EXERCISE SPIRITUAL

NUTRITION FAMILY / FRIENDS

HYDRATION SLEEP

INTENTIONAL
living

4 WEEK ASSESSMENT

CONGRATULATIONS! You have completed a 4-week cycle of your journey toward a more intentional life. Now it's time to take an assessment of that time and effort.

it is important to be honest with yourself and understand that this is a long term commitment, not just a short term goal to meet. Allow yourself some grace to grow and develop good practices, while acknowledging the challenges. Success will come in time and look like a healthier, happier you.

WHAT WENT WELL? _____

_____

_____

_____

WHAT WERE SOME CHALLENGES? _____

_____

_____

_____

_____

WHAT ARE SOME WAYS TO OVERCOME AT LEAST ONE CHALLENGE

GOING FORWARD? _____

_____

_____

_____

DID YOU SEE IMPROVEMENTS IN STRESS LEVELS

AND PRODUCTIVITY? _____

ANY ADDITIONAL NOTES AND THOUGHTS :

_____

_____

_____

_____

WHERE WILL YOU FOCUS YOUR INTENTIONS DURING

THE NEXT CYCLE? _____

_____

_____

AFFIRMATION OR QUOTE FOR INSPIRATION

KEEP UP THE GOOD WORK

INTENTIONAL
Living

FINAL ASSESSMENT

WELCOME to the year end assessment!

You should be so proud of yourself for accomplishing such an undertaking. The overall goal of this workbook is that you hopefully found that taking the time to live mindfully and with purpose is worth the effort. Being present in all of life's moments can result in more peace of mind, less stress and healthier habits. If these things developed gradually, came to you naturally, or even if you are still working toward your goals, it is important to see the potential in every single day and how you have the ability to really be present in your own life.

Please take a moment to reflect on the past year and identify what went well, what could have gone better, and what you will continue to do in order to live an intentional life.

Thank you so much for using this workbook on your journey, and best wishes for your continued success!

WHAT WERE YOUR STRENGTHS? _____

_____

_____

_____

_____

WHAT DID YOU FIND MOST CHALLENGING? _____

_____

_____

_____

_____

_____

WHAT SURPRISED YOU THE MOST ABOUT LIVING
AN INTENTIONAL LIFE? _____

_____
_____
_____
_____

WHAT OTHER PARTS OF YOUR LIFE ARE YOU READY TO ADD
MINDFULNESS TO? _____

_____
_____
_____
_____

ANY ADDITIONAL NOTES AND THOUGHTS :

_____
_____
_____
_____

HOW WILL YOU CONTINUE YOUR JOURNEY TO FIND AND ENJOY

INTENTIONAL MOMENTS IN LIFE? _____

_____
_____

AFFIRMATION OR QUOTE FOR INSPIRATION

INTENTIONAL
Living

Resources

THE FOLLOWING PAGES PROVIDE YOU WITH SOME IDEAS THAT CAN ADD INTENTIONALITY TO DIFFERENT PARTS OF YOUR LIFE.

USE WHAT YOU WANT AND TAKE THE SPACE PROVIDED AT THE BOTTOM OF EACH PAGE TO ADD MORE IDEAS AS THEY COME TO YOU FOR FUTURE REFERENCE.

THE
INTENTIONAL
Living
WORKBOOK

HABIT

28 27 26 25 24 23 22 21 20 19 18 17 16 15 14 13 12 11 10 9 8 7 6 5 4 3 2 1

HABIT

28 27 26 25 24 23 22 21 20 19 18 17 16 15 14 13 12 11 10 9 8 7 6 5 4 3 2 1

LIFE BALANCE

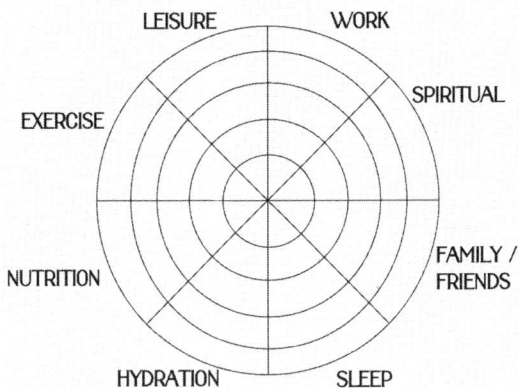

LIFE BALANCE

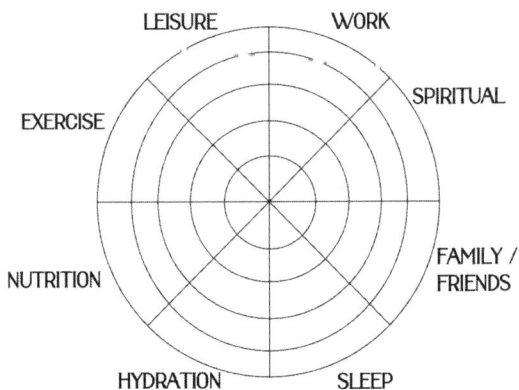

LIFE BALANCE

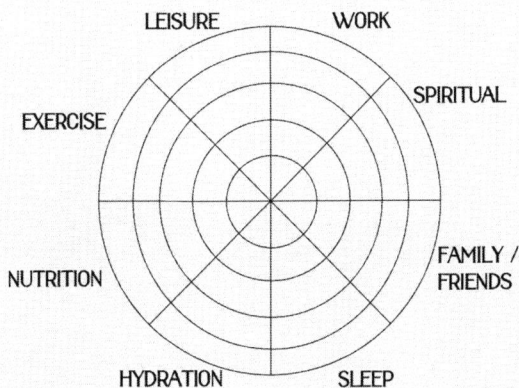

FAMILY & FRIENDS

CALL A FRIEND YOU HAVEN'T SEEN IN A WHILE AND MAKE A COFFEE/LUNCH DATE

ORGANIZE A GAME NIGHT

MAKE A FAVORITE FAMILY MEAL OR GO TO A FAVORITE RESTAURANT

PROVIDE YOUR FULL ATTENTION WHEN TOGETHER WITH OTHERS

TAKE TIME AT REGULAR INTERVALS TO SPEND MEANINGFUL TIME WITH YOUR SIGNIFICANT OTHER. THIS CAN BE EVERY MORNING FOR COFFEE OR FINDING SOMETHING EACH MONTH IN YOUR COMMUNITY TO EXPERIENCE.

CREATE A SCHEDULE FOR YOUR FAMILY'S ACTIVITIES AND LIFE REQUIREMENTS EVERY MONTH TO AVOID CONFLICTS AND CHAOS. TAKE TIME AND CARE TO IDENTIFY AREAS THAT NEED TO BE STREAMLINED, PRIORITIZED, OR ELIMINATED.

ELIMINATE ELECTRONIC DEVICES AT THE DINNER TABLE OR DURING FAMILY TIME

DO NOT MISTAKE SOCIAL MEDIA FOR MEANINGFUL INTERACTION. USE THOSE TOOLS AS QUICK WAYS OF STAYING CONNECTED, BUT ESTABLISH REAL CONNECTIONS IN THE REAL WORLD.

BE HONEST WITH RELATIONSHIPS THAT ARE ONE-SIDED OR TOXIC TO YOUR MENTAL HEALTH. MAKE ACTION STEPS TO RESOLVE THE ISSUE OR REMOVE YOURSELF FROM THE EMOTIONAL TURMOIL

ADD MORE IDEAS BELOW:

SPIRITUALITY

FIND A QUIET PLACE IN YOUR HOME AND SET ASIDE TIME DAILY TO SPEND IN PRAYER OR MEDITATION

VOLUNTEER AT A LOCAL CHURCH OR OTHER HOUSE OF WORSHIP

ATTEND RELIGIOUS SERVICES REGULARLY

READ A DAILY DEVOTIONAL OR AFFIRMATION, AND REFLECT ON THE IMPACT OF THE MESSAGE

PLAN A TRIP TO A SPIRITUALLY SIGNIFICANT PLACE

WRITE IN A JOURNAL ABOUT YOUR THOUGHTS AND SPIRITUAL JOURNEY

BE MINDFUL OF OTHERS WHO MAY HOLD DIFFERENT BELIEFS OR IDEAS AND LET YOUR INTERACTIONS BE PEACEFUL. SHOW HOW YOUR INTENTIONALITY REFLECTS YOUR VALUES

FIND A CHARITY THAT SHARES YOUR RELIGIOUS BELIEFS OR ALIGNS WITH YOUR VALUES AND SUPPORT THEIR MISSION TO HELP OTHERS, EITHER FINANCIALLY OR THROUGH VOLUNTEERING

LISTEN TO AN UPLIFTING OR SPIRITUALLY MOTIVATING PODCAST OR SPEAKER

PICK ONE OF THE 5 REIKI PRINCIPLES TO PRACTICE DURING THE DAY:

     1 JUST FOR TODAY, I WILL NOT WORRY

     2 JUST FOR TODAY, I WILL NOT BE ANGRY

     3 JUST FOR TODAY, I WILL BE GRATEFUL

     4 JUST FOR TODAY, I WILL DO MY WORK HONESTLY

     5 JUST FOR TODAY, I WILL BE KIND TO EVERY LIVING THING

ADD MORE IDEAS BELOW:

WORK

SET ALARM FOR 10 MINUTES EARLIER IN THE MORNING TO AVOID RUSHING THROUGH THE MORNING ROUTINE

PRE-PLAN MEALS FOR THE NEXT DAY TO ENSURE A HEALTHY BREAKFAST AND LUNCH

SPEAK KIND WORDS TO THREE PEOPLE THROUGHOUT THE DAY

REMOVE DISTRACTIONS WHEN INTERACTING WITH ANOTHER PERSON OR IN A GROUP SETTING (PROVIDE YOUR FULL ATTENTION)

CREATE ACTION STEPS TO INCREASE FINANCIAL INTENTIONALITY SO THAT THE MONEY YOU ARE WORKING FOR HAS A PURPOSE – DEVELOP A BUDGET, AVOID IMPULSE PURCHASES, MAKE MANAGEABLE FINANCIAL GOALS, OR SET ASIDE DONATIONS TO CHARITIES OF YOUR CHOICE

DEVELOP AN ORGANIZATION SYSTEM FOR THE THINGS YOU NEED DURING THE DAY

ESTABLISH A CUT-OFF TIME IN THE EVENING FOR WORK-RELATED ACTIVITIES

BE MINDFUL ABOUT CHECKING EMAILS OR TAKING CALLS DURING FAMILY OR SELF CARE TIME

BE OPEN TO NEW OPPORTUNITIES

DEVELOP A SCRIPT ON HOW TO SAY "NO" TO REQUESTS THAT YOU CANNOT OR DO NOT WANT TO COMMIT YOUR TIME AND ENERGY TO AT THIS TIME

ADD MORE IDEAS BELOW:

LEISURE & SELF-CARE

DANCE TO YOUR FAVORITE MUSIC

SET ASIDE TIME TO READ FOR ENJOYMENT

PLAN A ROAD TRIP

MAKE YOUR FAVORITE HOT BEVERAGE

START WORKING ON A NEW SKILL OR HOBBY

UNPLUG FROM SOCIAL MEDIA

TURN OFF UNNECESSARY PHONE NOTIFICATIONS

START A GRATITUDE JOURNAL

MAKE A DIGITAL OR PHYSICAL VISION BOARD FOR YOUR FUTURE GOALS IN LIFE (SIX MONTHS, ONE YEAR OR FIVE YEARS)

CREATE A MORNING AND EVENING ROUTINE TO FOLLOW THAT ALLOWS FOR SMALL MOMENTS OF SELF CARE, LIKE 5 MINUTES OF STRETCHING IN THE MORNING OR USING AN INDULGENT MOISTURIZER OR CLEANSER AT NIGHT

MAKE A LIST OF GO-TO BOOKS, MOVIES, MUSIC, OR WEBSITES THAT INSPIRE YOU OR MAKE YOU HAPPY. REFER TO THAT LIST WHEN YOU NEED A MOOD BOOST AND HAVE THE TIME TO RELAX

ADD MORE IDEAS BELOW:

EXERCISE

COMMIT TO A SET AMOUNT OF PHYSICAL ACTIVITY EVERY DAY (START SLOW AND WORK UP TO YOUR OPTIMUM ACTIVITY LEVEL IF THIS IS A CHALLENGE) REMEMBER TO INCORPORATE TIME FOR WARM UP AND COOL DOWN

START A NEW STYLE OF PHYSICAL ACTIVITY THAT YOU ARE CURIOUS ABOUT

MAKE A LIST OF NON-CONVENTIONAL EXERCISE ACTIVITIES TO TRY WHEN YOU ARE FEELING LIKE A CHANGE (DANCING, LANDSCAPING/GARDENING, REARRANGING FURNITURE, ICE SKATING, RAKING LEAVES, WASHING THE CAR … SO MANY IDEAS)

TAKE A HIKE EITHER ALONE OR WITH A FRIEND/FAMILY

BE MINDFUL AND LISTEN TO YOUR BODY AS YOU MOVE THROUGH EXERCISE ACTIVITIES. THIS CAN BE ATTENTION TO DISCOMFORT OR FEELING TENSION RELEASE, SO PAY ATTENTION TO ALL SENSATIONS BOTH GOOD AND BAD.

PRACTICE MINI EXERCISES, LIKE CALF LIFTS, PLANKS OR SQUATS, THROUGHOUT THE DAY IN BETWEEN OTHER ACTIVITIES

ELIMINATE NEGATIVE SELF TALK – MAKE A LIST OF POSITIVE AFFIRMATIONS ABOUT YOUR FITNESS JOURNEY AND REFER TO THIS LIST ANY TIME YOU NOTICE NEGATIVE THOUGHTS ARISE

SPONSOR A CHILD IN HIS/HER CHOSEN SPORT (EQUIPMENT OR ENTRANCE FEES) TO SHARE THE GIFT OF PHYSICAL ACTIVITY WITH OTHERS

NOTE: AS WITH ANY EXERCISE PROGRAM CONSULT A TRUSTED MEDICAL PROFESSIONAL BEFORE MAKING CHANGES OR STARTING A NEW ROUTINE ALL IDEAS PRESENTED HERE ARE FOR INFORMATIONAL PURPOSES ONLY.

ADD MORE IDEAS BELOW:

NUTRITION

MEAL PLAN FOR THE UPCOMING WEEK TO AVOID LAST MINUTE CONVENIENCE MEALS

COMMIT TO EATING THREE HEALTHY MEALS DURING THE DAY

PACK YOUR LUNCH RATHER THAN GRABBING CONVENIENCE FOOD

CUT ONE UNHEALTHY FOOD CHOICE FROM YOUR DIET

TAKE YOUR VITAMINS

MAKE A GROCERY LIST AND STICK TO IT WHEN AT THE STORE

TRY ONE NEW HEALTHY RECIPE THIS WEEK

ADD FRESH FOODS TO YOUR DIET

BE MINDFUL OF THE FLAVORS AND TEXTURES OF YOUR FOOD AS YOU EAT & ENJOY THOSE MOMENTS

IDENTIFY AND ELIMINATE AN UNHEALTHY LIFESTYLE CHOICE ASSOCIATED WITH FOOD. SUCH AS EATING WHEN BORED OR HAVING MEALS IN FRONT OF THE TV

BE MINDFUL OF WHEN YOU ARE FULL AND STOP EATING AT THAT POINT

SUPPORT YOUR LOCAL FOOD BANK OR OTHER CHARITY THAT PROVIDES FOOD TO THOSE IN NEED

NOTE: AS WITH ANY DIET PROGRAM, CONSULT A TRUSTED MEDICAL PROFESSIONAL BEFORE MAKING CHANGES OR STARTING A NEW NUTRITION ROUTINE. ALL IDEAS PRESENTED HERE ARE FOR INFORMATIONAL PURPOSES ONLY.

ADD MORE IDEAS BELOW:

HYDRATION

COMMIT TO DRINKING A CERTAIN AMOUNT OF WATER EACH DAY (START LOW AND WORK YOUR WAY UP TO OPTIMUM PERSONAL LEVELS OVER TIME IF THIS IS A CHALLENGE)

TAKE A REUSABLE WATER BOTTLE WITH YOU DURING THE DAY AND REFILL IT

ELIMINATE SINGLE USE PLASTIC WATER BOTTLES

ADD FRUIT OR OTHER INFUSIONS TO YOUR WATER FOR VARIETY

ENJOY A CUP OF HOT TEA IN THE EVENING

DRINK A GLASS OF WATER ABOUT HALF AN HOUR BEFORE YOUR MEALS

CUT BACK ON CAFFEINATED DRINKS (GREEN TEA CAN BE A REPLACEMENT IF YOU NEED THE BOOST)

SET A PHONE ALERT FOR EVERY HOUR OR TWO TO HYDRATE IF YOU NEED THE REMINDER

EAT FOODS WITH A HIGH WATER CONTENT, LIKE PINEAPPLES, WATERMELON OR CUCUMBERS

CONSIDER SUPPORTING CLEAN WATER INITIATIVES THAT PROVIDE DRINKING WATER TO AREAS IN NEED

ADD MORE IDEAS BELOW:

SLEEP

GO TO BED ONE HALF HOUR EARLIER

DISCONTINUE USE OF ELECTRONIC DEVICES AN HOUR BEFORE GOING TO BED

INVEST IN COMFORTABLE BEDDING

MAKE YOUR BEDROOM A SANCTUARY – NICE LIGHTING, NO DISTRACTIONS, & COZY FURNISHINGS

SET YOUR ALARM FOR WHEN YOU NEED TO GET UP, NOT FOR HITTING SNOOZE

PRACTICE MIND CALMING TECHNIQUES FOR FALLING ASLEEP

DO NOT CHECK SOCIAL MEDIA OR NEWS BEFORE OR IN BED

DEVELOP AN EVENING ROUTINE THAT TRAINS YOUR MIND FOR SLEEP

DRINK A WARM NON-CAFFEINATED TEA OR MILK BEFORE RETIRING TO BED

END YOUR DAY WITH TIME SPENT IN QUIET REFLECTION OR PRAYER

WRITE A FEW MINUTES IN A GRATITUDE JOURNAL BEFORE LIGHTS OUT

ADD A CALMING SCENT, LIKE LAVENDER TO YOUR BEDTIME ROUTINE

ADD MORE IDEAS BELOW:

NOTES

NOTES

NOTES

NOTES

NOTES

Made in the USA
Middletown, DE
07 September 2021